DOUGH CREATIONS

FOOD TO FOLK ART

Also by the authors

START OFF IN DOUGH CRAFT

DOUGH CREATIONS

FOOD TO FOLK ART

Pat Gardner • Kay Gleason

Chilton Book Company   Radnor, Pennsylvania

Copyright © 1977 by Pat Gardner and Kay Gleason
All Rights Reserved
Published in Radnor, Pa., by Chilton Book Company
and simultaneously in Don Mills, Ont., Canada,
by Thomas Nelson & Sons, Ltd.
All projects, unless otherwise credited,
were made by the authors
Manufactured in the United States of America

Library of Congress Cataloging in Publication Data
Gardner, Pat.
   Dough creations.

   (Chilton's creative crafts series)
   1. Bread dough craft. 2. Dough.
I. Gleason, Kay, joint author. II. Title.
TT880.G37   745.5   77-4588
ISBN 0-8019-6376-1
ISBN 0-8019-6377-X pbk.

1 2 3 4 5 6 7 8 9 0   5 4 3 2 1 0 9 8 7

Contents

Introduction

Fig. I-1 Hessian soldier.
From a gingerbread mold.

Breads of symbolism and celebration abound the world over and are part of almost every cultural heritage. Wedding breads, fertility loaves, and bread for the dead all typify the manner in which bread has mirrored a people's rituals, attitudes, and deepest desires.

The use of bread dough as an artistic medium is rooted deep in our religious and social traditions. The ancient cultures of Egypt, Greece, Rome, and Latin America are echoed in our contemporary approach to bread as both food and folk art. Bread, as a symbol and as sustenance, has changed little over the centuries. And perhaps we have not changed so much, either.

Breads and cookies, sculpted and decorated according to timeless tradition or individual imagination, satisfy the creative urge and the palate. And from its traditional beginnings, bread dough, with its many variations, has found its place in the contemporary craft resurgence in this country. Baker's clay and other inedible doughs have been enthusiastically welcomed by all who are fascinated by the simplicity and artistic potential of craft doughs. Moreover, working with craft dough is inexpensive and requires no special equipment—it borrows its ingredients from the kitchen and its textures and ornamentation from the vast array of objects with which we live.

Dough is utilized as an artistic vehicle on a wide range of levels and in varying degrees of technical complexity. School children are delighted by its tactile properties and its spontaneous simplicity. Studio craftsmen are intrigued and challenged in that it is a basic and direct medium, yet one with great potential for exploration. Most of us stand somewhere between the fresh, unchanneled expression of the child and the serious approach of the studio artist, and enjoy the craft of bread on our own ground. Even simple ornamentation becomes a joy when it is the work of our own hands.

It is our aim to illustrate the versatility and artistic capability of this craft medium.

Part I

BREADS AND SWEETS

Chapter 1

History

Tracing the history of bread can be as vividly revealing of man's development as are his art treasures and documents. Indeed, grain and bread may figure even more frequently than artifacts in the archeological remains of past cultures. Thousands of years ago, hunters carried wild grains for sustenance on nomadic journeys. As the techniques of cultivation became known, man interrupted his wanderings to form infant agricultural societies in what is now thought to be the cradle of wheat, Abyssinia. The harvested grains and seeds were ground on small rubbing stones. Combined with water, this sun-dried mash formed the crude beginnings of bread.

Lake Dwellers of Switzerland added to that ancient recipe by baking their hard, crusty flatbreads on hot stones. Mexican tortillas, Indian chapati, New England johnny cakes, and Chinese pao ping all echo that primary food of 8,000 years ago.

The art of bread-baking was elevated dramatically with the Egyptian discovery of leavening. It is said that a forgetful slave set aside a batch of wheat flour dough which fermented and rose. Undaunted, he baked this peculiar puffy mass and presented mankind with a leavened loaf.

Another development was the baking of raw grains, sprouted in water by an open fire, into loaves. The loaves were broken up and soaked, and the mixture was allowed to ferment for a day. The liquor that was strained off was Egyptian beer, and its skimmed foam was used to ferment dough.

Leavened bread profoundly captured the imaginations of its creators. It was endowed with a mystique that lay deeply em-

3

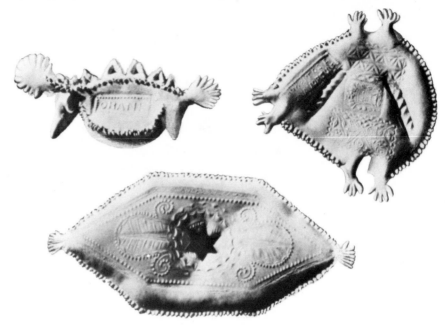

Fig. 1-2 Flatbreads from Sardinia in traditional designs. *Courtesy* Domus *Magazine, Milan, Italy.*

bedded in the religious, social, and creative traditions of many civilizations. Bakers in Egyptian society were as highly regarded as priests, and the baking furnaces were often built in temples. Tomb scenes depict the milling and making of breadstuffs and show men with long poles trampling the dough rather than kneading it. Paintings of conical-shaped loaves on altars reveal the early sacrificial uses made of bread that would be ritualistically repeated for centuries. Fish, bird, and animal "cookies," colored with earth pigments or sprinkled with seeds, were left in tombs for the dead spirits to enjoy. The ancient kitchen had found not only a form of religious expression but an art form as well.

Egyptian bread stalls offered the passer-by grain pastes, but the wealthy could choose from as many as forty varieties of baked fare. Round, flat, plaited, some were sweetened with honey and eggs, some flavored with camphor and sprinkled with poppy seeds and sesame. The finest loaves in the ancient world were baked in Egypt's beehive ovens. Egyptians watching the doughy lumps go into the oven and the puffy browned loaves emerge marveled at the magic spirits at work inside that caused such splendid transformations.

As bread's role in Egyptian society grew in significance, the government leapt in to control the granaries, creating a great dependence of the people on the state for food. Egyptians received "daily bread"—grains and loaves and beer—in payment for a day's labor, three breads and two jugs being an average day's wages. The "number of breads" one possessed signified his financial status. Ovens were virtually mints and flour baked in them became coins.

By the fourth century BC, the Greeks had forged the first mill and baked an endless variety of loaves, cakes, and cookies. Marvelously heat-retentive kettle ovens baked loaves flavored with salt and cheese, and mushroom-shaped *Cappadocia*. Bread was considered sacred and was enshrouded in Grecian spiritual mysteries, and the Bread Church of Eleusis arose in celebration of it. Profound and solemn legends grew around it. Grains were milled and transformed into plow-shaped wheat and honey cakes, worshipful gifts to set before Demeter, the goddess of grain and fertility. It was she, according to mythology, who gave the first grain to Triptolemus and instructed him to cover the earth with its blessing.

As Romans absorbed the culture of ancient Greece, they zealously welcomed baking and milling into their home kitchens. Bread was first baked in Roman homes by conquered Greek slaves who were knowledgeable in baking hot fragrant delights. Eventually, however, demand for bread outdistanced production and commercial bakeries were born. A guild was established, and bakers, bound to their work under threat of punishment, enjoyed special privileges and living quarters. Bread stamps, carved of wood and stone, carried the baker's mark and branded the loaves against possible theft.

Baked in masonry chambers set over fire boxes, festive loaves shaped as wedding rings and a myriad of other images attest to Roman creativity. Bread retained its exalted position, and the goddess of grain, now called Ceres, was worshipped faithfully.

Rome's later nationalization of bakeries was an attempt to help relieve her increasing poverty. A law required bakers to furnish bread for the needy, and soon hundreds of thousands of Romans were receiving a bread and grain dole. The poor could not afford flour, yet wealthy Roman women powdered their noses with it. Feasts lasting for days on end and lives dedicated solely to food and pleasure weakened Rome's leaders. The bread riots that resulted from the unrest and dissatisfaction actually deposed emperors and were the igniting sparks for revolutions.

The Roman legions that conquered and occupied the huge empire carried with them the art and means of baking. Mills and ovens lugged along on campaigns brought to northern and western Europe the irresistible aroma of the freshly baked loaf. As the Roman Empire waned, however, regular grain shipments to the rest of Europe ceased and commercial baking disappeared.

The spread of Christianity had a profound effect upon bread's

Croissants, first baked in 1686, were a commemoration of a victory. Hungarian bakers working at night in Budapest heard the Turks tunneling under the city and spread the alarm. The invading Turks were repelled and the bakers were lauded for their vigilance. As a reward, the bakers were commissioned to create a new roll shaped as a crescent, the emblem of Turkey.

role in society and consummated the spiritual significance attached to it. Bread became a holy sacrament. Early Christians, instead of baking for pagan gods, fashioned loaves of celebration and thanks to serve at religious feasts and holidays.

During the Dark Ages, the intricacies of breadmaking were nurtured and practiced primarily in monasteries. As the towns and cities of medieval Europe began to mushroom and organize, baking emerged from its cloistered existence. Bakers' guilds were quickly reorganized under heavy-handed supervision. Everywhere in Europe strict codes of behavior governed the baker's actions. In London one especially devious baker made off with dough in spite of the watchfulness of a continuing stream of customers coming to have their own bread shaped and baked. He drilled a hole in the middle of his work table and hid a small member of his staff underneath. As each loaf was being kneaded, the hidden conspirator plucked bits of dough through the hole. The customer's loaf went into the oven unnoticeably lighter, and the day's collected dough was combined to form new loaves for public sale. The penalty for such misconduct was a trip for the baker through the streets of London wearing the offending loaves around his neck.

Bread was more than food. It had become the symbol of food. The Anglo-Saxon word "lord" actually means breadkeeper and "lady" translates, predictably, to breadmaker.

In some areas of medieval Europe, dough was spread as a table covering for dining nobles. These dough "cloths," soaked with spilled wine and splashed meat juices, were taken up after the meal and given to the servants. Bread also could serve as an absorbent plate, or "trencher." Two people shared a common food bowl and each spread his portion on thick slabs of stale, unleavened bread. These could either be eaten later or tossed to the waiting dogs.

Henry II, King of England, issued the "English Assize of Bread," which stipulated how breads would be distributed commercially. White bread was to be eaten exclusively by royalty and clergy. The middle classes were to eat white and whole wheat combinations, and "all inferior types of people" were left to the loaves made of whole bran. This law remained in effect for six centuries.

Medieval Europe doted on gingerbread, then a solid bread of honey, spices, and flour. Gilded with gold leaf and clove-studded, it often took the shape of a fleur-de-lis, a token from a lady to her favorite knight. Europeans extravagantly embellished bread. A dizzying display of baked artistry was witnessed by the rich and poor who gathered at the great fairs of Europe, the social events of the Middle Ages.

Italian artists responded to the need for mass production of diverse baked goods by fashioning molds cast in clay from metal and stone positives. Traveling merchants carried these elaborately patterned bread and marzipan molds throughout the country, enabling bakers to share their edible art with all Europe (figs. 1–3 and 1–4).

Intricately patterned and deliciously spiced honeycakes bearing stories, customs, and family symbols began falling from these molds into the hands of the common man. These artistic treasures were often preserved and displayed rather than eaten, and the molds from which they came are now museum masterpieces.

As in Egypt and Europe, bread rose to a position of exaltation and artistic expression in the ancient Incan civilization too. Corncake images representing humans and animals were symbolically sacrificed to pagan gods, and tiny breads strung as necklaces were used to decorate altars and prayer arrows. Later these figures were thought to possess health-giving qualities and were buried with the dead to be taken for sustenance on the journey into the next life.

The creation of intricate bread dough figures depicting camels-of-the-clouds (llamas), angels, and members of the Holy Family began with the Spanish Conquest. Indians in the area of Bolivia and Ecuador celebrated the new teachings of Christianity

Fig. 1–3 Man riding a rooster. From a medieval cookie mold.

Fig. 1–4 Cherubs hold aloft the sign of a gingerbread guild. From a medieval cookie mold.

Fig. 1–5 Antique handcarved speculaas mold. *Courtesy of William Bernhardt.*

Fig. 1–6 Earthenware Mexican idol wears thick heishe necklace. The beads are made of breadcrumb dough.

by imitating in dough the religious figures introduced by the Conquistadores.

In the New World, colonists arriving on the eastern shores of America found corn to be a more cooperative crop than the grains to which they were accustomed. Thus wheat flour, a scarcity at first, was saved for the bread of gentlemen and was mostly put aside for birthdays and holidays.

Cornpone, a modern palatable form of grain paste, was baked on a warm hearth and considered to be the best bread on which to work and travel. Johnny cakes, originally called journeycakes, were tucked into pilgrim pockets for portable sustenance. Such colonial bread fare as holy pokes, jolly boys, featherbeds, and popdoodle reflect a New England baking philosophy laced with spirit and humor.

Hardtacks and sourdoughs accompanied the pioneers as they nudged our frontiers to the sea. Baking was done at fireside in heavy skillets or portable ovens until the appearance of the iron stove in the middle of the last century.

And so the colonists and pioneers had their own ways with bread, creating new loaves to add to the familiar customs of the Old World. This kitchen marriage of old and new has created a baking tradition that liberally represents most of the world's bread-baking peoples.

Fig. 2–1 French bread alligators holding sugar frogs in their jaws. *Baked by Chef Les Molnar.*

Chapter 2

Sculptured Breads

Rolling pin, flour, and yeast . . . materials for a sculptor? Not the marble and chisel of a Michelangelo certainly, but a sculptural medium nevertheless. Dough has been kneaded and molded into likenesses of animals, people, and places since Egyptians fashioned the first leavened loaves for the sustenance of their dead in the next life.

The bakers' guilds of the Middle Ages found bread sculpture an exciting medium for portraying the people, events, and fancies of a century. The baker had become a sculptor, forming breads into elaborate shapes that often carried ancient symbolic meanings. Picture breads (*gebildbrote*) were sculptures depicting horses, serpents, sheaves of harvest, fish and fowl, and Christian symbols. White bread, being of the finest texture and highest rise, was used exclusively in Europe for the oven creations which were sometimes as complex as depictions of the Garden of Eden.

Bread sculpture is on the rise in America. Artists and craftspeople, as well as homemakers and children, are all participating in this fragrantly satisfying occupation. Loaves appear as mermaids and dolphins (see fig. 2–2), whales and snails, lions and lambs in biblical repose—all expressions of a society returning to the primary pleasures of creating food and art with one's own hands.

Jewish holy days and festivals are rich in bread traditions. Every Sabbath table bears two loaves called challah, *served in remembrance of the double portion of manna which God gave the Israelites for the Sabbath during the forty years of wandering in the wilderness.*

On Rosh Hashanah, challah is embellished with birds and ladders baked on top to carry the family's prayers to heaven.

10

Fig. 2–2 Triton bread
sculpture.

BRIOCHE LAMB

Brioche, a bread of French origin, is made from a light, eggy
yeast dough. It dates back hundreds of years and is traditionally
round with a little topknot. In recent years, however, it has
been known to assume any number of fanciful disguises. An extremely cooperative sculpting dough, brioche can be risen,
punched down and risen again any number of times with no ill
effect. Its puffing seems to know no bounds and you will see
your designs "grow" before your eyes. Sometimes it seems to
have a mind and imagination of its own. Better to let it rise only
a few minutes after that final shaping—it will go right on rising
in the oven.

To take a freshly baked loaf to breakfast, shape your dough
sculpture one day and hold it overnight, unbaked, in the refrigerator. Bake it as usual in the morning (it will have risen suf-
ficiently in the refrigerator). The baked sculpture also freezes
well and can be reheated in foil in a 350° oven. It is also delicious served cold.

Pass the brioche and let everyone tear off a piece rather than
cut it. Delicately flavored with a hint of orange peel, brioche is especially nice served with sweet (unsalted) butter or
Camembert cheese.

Fig. 2–3 Brioche lamb.

Recipe

1 package yeast	2 teaspoons vanilla
¼ cup warm water	½ teaspoon salt
⅓ cup milk	3 whole eggs
½ cup butter	3 egg yolks
½ cup sugar	4½ to 5 cups white flour
2 tablespoons grated orange	beaten egg white
peel	

Stir the yeast into the warm water and set it aside to soften. Heat the milk to scalding and cool to lukewarm. In a large bowl, cream the butter, sugar, orange peel, vanilla, and salt until fluffy. Beat in the eggs and yolks, one at a time. Add the milk and yeast. Gradually beat in the flour. Turn the soft dough onto a well-floured board and knead vigorously until it is soft and elastic, about 10 to 15 minutes.

Put the dough in a large greased bowl, turning once to grease the top. Cover the bowl and set it in a warm place for about one hour or until the dough has doubled in bulk.

To shape the lamb: Punch the dough down and knead it to remove the bubbles. Pull off about ¼ of the dough and put it aside to use for the lamb's features. On a greased baking sheet, form the large portion of the dough into a smooth round shape and pat it to about 12″ across to form the body of the lamb. Flatten a fist-sized ball of dough for the lamb's face and walnut-sized balls for the ears and legs. Moisten the areas where these features will be joined with a bit of water on your finger tips. Press the face, ears, and legs onto the lamb's body (fig. 2–4). Roll little bits of dough for the eyelashes, cheeks, and nose. Position these on the face. Roll little balls of dough into ropes to form the curls of lamb's wool. Coil these all over the lamb's body.

Allow the completed shape (fig. 2–5) to rise in a warm place just until it is slightly puffed looking, maybe only 10 minutes. It will go right on puffing in the oven. Brush it gently with the beaten egg white and bake it in a 350° oven for 45 minutes or until it is richly browned.

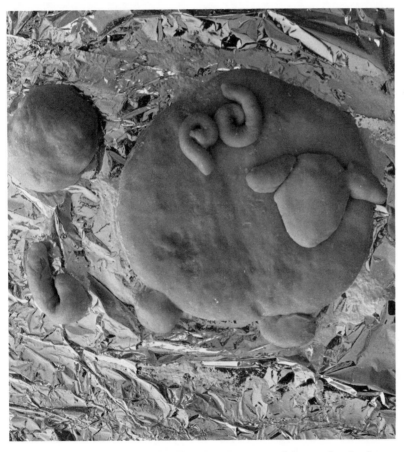

Fig. 2–4 Pieces of dough form the lamb's face, ears, and feet, and coils of dough are positioned to form "wool."

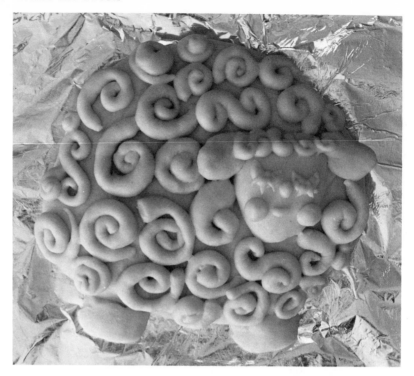

Fig. 2–5 The shaped lamb is left to puff for a few minutes before baking.

MUSHROOM BREAD

The classical Greeks made a mushroom-shaped bread that they called Cappadocia. It was soft and salty and sprinkled with poppy seeds. This modern-day version (fig. 2–6) may well retain some of the character of that fourth-century BC bread in that it is also mildly salty and mushroom shaped. The mushroom flavor of the loaf comes as a bonus. The recipe makes four loaves.

Recipe

¼ cup margarine or butter	½ cup warm water
½ pound mushrooms, chopped fine	2 packages active dry yeast
1 cup onion, chopped fine	1 egg
2 cups milk	1 cup wheat germ
3 tablespoons molasses	4 to 5 cups flour (combination of white and whole wheat)
2 teaspoons salt	
¼ teaspoon pepper	

Melt 2 tablespoons of the margarine or butter in a large skillet. Add the mushrooms and onion and sauté until the onion is tender and the liquid has evaporated. Cool.

Scald the milk and stir in the molasses, salt, and pepper. Cool

Fig. 2–6 Cappadocia. Sautéed mushrooms and onion give extra flavor to this modern-day version of a Greek classic.

to lukewarm. Sprinkle the yeast over the warm water in a large bowl. Stir to dissolve. Add the warm milk mixture, the mushroom and onion mixture, egg, wheat germ, and 2 cups of the flour. Stir in enough additional flour to make a stiff dough.

Turn the dough out onto a lightly floured board. Knead it until it is smooth and elastic, probably 8 to 10 minutes. Place it in a greased bowl, turning once to grease the top. Cover and let it rise in a warm place until it is double in bulk, about an hour.

As the dough is rising, prepare the mushroom baking pans, below.

Mushroom Baking Pans

4 30-ounce fruit or vegetable cans
4 heavy cardboard squares, 2″ wider than the can openings
aluminum foil

Trace the can openings on the center of the squares; cut them out and discard the circles. Cover the cardboard collars with foil and place them tightly over the openings of the cans. Grease the cans and the foil collars.

When the dough has risen, divide it into four equal pieces. Shape each piece into a round ball. Place each of these balls into a prepared mushroom pan. Let the dough rise until it is doubled again, about one hour. Preheat the oven to 350°. With your

Vasilopitta, *a Greek New Year's bread served just at the stroke of midnight, contains a coin that will bring prosperity to its lucky finder. Named for St. Basil, Vasilopitta can take various forms: a sweetbread, an oversized flat cookie, or an elaborate cake.*

finger tips, gently press the lower edge of the mushroom cap down onto the foil-covered collar. Reshape the cap if it needs it. Bake mushroom loaves about 40 minutes or until done (crust should be golden brown). Remove from the pans and cool on wire racks. Butter the caps while warm and sprinkle with poppy seeds.

WHEAT SHEAF BREAD

Wheat sheaf bread (fig. 2–16) is a particularly nutritious loaf . . . and it's delicious. The recipe makes two loaves.

Recipe

1½ cups milk	½ cup warm water
⅓ cup butter	2 packages active dry
2 tablespoons honey	yeast
2 tablespoons molasses	2 cups whole wheat flour
1½ teaspoons salt	¼ cup wheat germ
2 large shredded-wheat biscuits, crushed	2 to 3 cups white flour

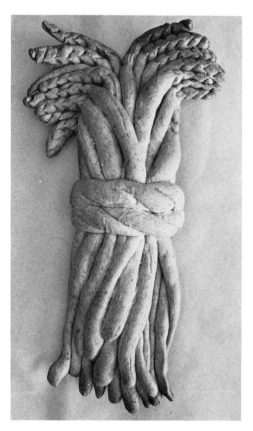

Sooth-saying qualities attributed to bread centuries ago live strongly in the traditions of the Scandinavian countries. Three straws from the harvest were baked in a loaf. If that loaf cracked during storage, poor crops could be expected. Breads that developed fissures during cutting hinted that death lurked. A loaf with a candle in it, or weighted with mercury, was floated on the water to find drowned bodies.

Fig. 2–7 Wheat sheaf bread.

Scald the milk. Stir in butter, honey, molasses, salt, and the crushed shredded-wheat biscuits. Cool this mixture to luke-warm.

Sprinkle the yeast over the warm water in a large bowl. Stir to dissolve the yeast. Mix the yeast mixture and the whole wheat flour, and beat until smooth. Stir in the wheat germ and add enough white flour to make a stiff dough.

Turn the dough out onto a lightly floured board and knead it until it is smooth and elastic, about 10 minutes. Place the dough in a greased bowl, turning once to grease the top. Cover lightly and let rise in a warm place until doubled in bulk, about one hour. Punch the dough down.

Divide half the dough into 18 equal pieces. Roll two pieces into 12" ropes. Twist the ropes and set them aside. Roll four pieces into 18" ropes. Place one 18" rope lengthwise on the center of a greased baking sheet, bending the top third of the rope off to the left at a 45° angle. Place another 18" rope on the sheet next to and touching the first rope, but bend the top third off to the right. Repeat this procedure using two more 18" ropes, placing them and shaping them so that the ropes are touching.

Roll the remaining pieces into 15" ropes. Arrange them on top of and around the 18" ropes (see fig. 2–16). Spread out the ropes to form the bottom of the sheaf. Arrange the 12" twists side by side around the center of the sheaf, tucking the ends under.

Let the dough rise for the second time. Make final details by snipping diagonally with scissors along the bent portion of the stalks above the twists.

EASTER BREAD RABBITS

Rich, eggy breads bright with colored eggs celebrate Easter in most countries along the Mediterranean shores and as faraway as Brazil and as near as America. A Greek custom, the baking of thick, round loaves decorated with eggs, carries deep religious symbolism. The eggs, traditionally bright red to symbolize Christ's blood, were dyed only on Holy Thursday and Saturday and were tokens of good luck in the homes. Now frosted, glazed, or sesame-sprinkled braided loaves, entwining eggs tinted with the brightest colors of spring, are found on Easter morning on tables around the world.

The recipe below makes eight Easter bread rabbits like the one shown in fig. 2–8.

Fig. 2–8 Easter bread rabbit.

Recipe

8	eggs in shell, uncooked	2	packages active dry yeast
	Easter egg dye or food coloring	½	cup warm water (110°–115°)
½	cup milk	2	eggs, slightly beaten
½	cup sugar	1	teaspoon cinnamon
1	teaspoon salt	½	teaspoon nutmeg
½	cup shortening	4½	cups sifted flour
	grated peel of 2 lemons	1	egg, beaten

Hot cross buns, English rolls traditionally served on Good Friday, once bore prehistoric pagan symbols for sun and fire. Christians reworked the symbols to represent the cross, and baked the buns for feasts and celebrations.

Wash the 8 uncooked eggs, tint them with egg coloring, and set them aside. Scald the milk and add sugar, salt, shortening, and lemon peel. Cool this mixture to lukewarm. Sprinkle the yeast over the warm water and stir to dissolve. Add it to the milk mixture with the 2 beaten eggs, the cinnamon and nutmeg, and 2½ cups of flour. Beat until smooth. Stir in enough of the remaining flour, a little at a time, to form a dough that is easy to handle.

Turn dough out onto a lightly floured board and knead until it is smooth and elastic. Place the dough in a lightly greased bowl, turning it once to grease the top. Cover and let rise in a warm place free from drafts until doubled in size, about one hour.

Punch the dough down, cover it, and let it rise again until almost doubled, about 30 minutes.

Divide the dough into 8 equal parts. Form each part into a rabbit, as follows (refer to fig. 2–8 as needed).

Working on a separate piece of foil for each rabbit, form an oval-shaped piece of dough for the body. Cut a separation in the lower ¼ of the piece to form legs. Shape feet. Mold a round ball for the head. Add ears and give them a jaunty angle. Press tiny balls of dough for eyes onto the face. A little nose and whiskers complete the features. Press an uncooked, dyed Easter egg into the middle of the rabbit. (These eggs bake in the oven and taste like hardboiled ones.) Add a paw on either side of the egg to "hold" it.

Let the dough rise a few minutes until slightly puffed. Gently brush the figures with beaten egg white and bake in a 350° oven until golden brown, about 20 minutes.

PRETZELS

Pretzels, fat salty knots imitating praying arms, date back to the Middle Ages and were baked during Lent when the use of dairy products was prohibited. A long roll of dough twisted into the shape of a loose knot or the letter *B*, these flour and water bread sticks became popular in central Europe. The pretzel bakers of Vienna have a pretzel in their coat of arms to commemorate their turning back of the Turks in the siege of Vienna in 1510. In many European countries, a gilt pretzel hanging over a door indicates a bakery.

Pretzels, whose name is thought to have come from the Middle Latin word *bracciatello* ("little arms"), were brought to

Fig. 2–9 Pretzel. The name of these fat, salty knots comes from the word *bracciatello*, meaning "little arms."

America early in the colonization. Court records reveal their being sold to the Indians by 1652, probably resulting in their nickname, "Pilgrim's tokens."

This recipe makes one dozen soft, chewy pretzels, about 6″ wide.

Recipe

1¼ cups warm water	1 egg yolk
1 cake compressed yeast	1½ tablespoons water
½ teaspoon sugar	coarsely ground salt
4½ cups flour	

Mix the water, yeast, and sugar and let stand for one hour. Combine this mixture with the flour. Knead the dough for 8 or 9 minutes. Place it in a greased bowl, turn it over to grease the top, and let rise until it has doubled in bulk.

Divide the dough into 12 equal pieces. Roll each piece into a long fat coil and shape it into a pretzel. Place the pretzels on a greased baking sheet. Make a wash of the egg yolk and water, and brush each pretzel with it. Sprinkle the pretzels liberally with coarsely ground salt and allow them to rise again until they are almost, but not quite, double in bulk.

Bake them in a preheated oven at 475° for about 10 minutes or until rich brown. For a zesty snack, dip the pretzels into hot mustard.

SCULPTURED ETHNIC BREADS

Special traditions of breadmaking exist in almost every country. Some of those traditions are described and illustrated below, from the fanciful Sardinian bread creatures, to Mexico's *pan de muerto,* to America's prized sourdough. You can apply some of the ideas to your own breadmaking, or look to your family or regional history for your own traditions, or make up your own distinctive designs. The basic idea, of course, is very simple—special occasions deserve to be commemorated in a special bread.

Most firm loaf or flat breads are amenable to shaping, sculpting, clipping, or stamping. Or try the pretzel dough or any of the other bread recipes given previously in this chapter. Let your first experiments consist of simple designs, and then get as intricate and fanciful as you wish.

Sardinian Breads

Weddings and other feast days in Sardinia are an occasion for baking breads of extraordinary imagination and beauty. The

Fig. 2–10 Straw flowers and dried grass are combined with a gingham bow on this bread dough wreath. With a clear protective coating it will last many seasons. *Jan and Charles Hutchins.*

women exhibit in their breadmaking the same meticulous crafts-manship as in their woven-wool artistry and an artistic skill equal to that of their men who work iron and silver from the ancient mines in the mountains.

The breads from each province are distinctive. Some are shaped with horns, crests, and multiple heads, like small toasted creatures escaped from mythology (fig.2–11*a*). Other islanders stamp and bake puffed cushion-like breads as beautifully de-signed as the needlework produced in medieval cloisters (fig. 2–11*b*). Flat breads are carved and clipped with scissors and knives, then tied with ribbons of brocade (fig. 2–11*c*) and often hang on the walls of Sardinian homes.

Twice-baked breads from Nuovo province, made in extremely varied circular shapes, are sometimes as large as twenty-four inches across, providing a feast for shepherds in the fields.

Breads Baked for the Dead

Breads have always been baked to honor the dead and pay homage to ancestors. A mummified Egyptian was believed to have as his primary goal the return to mortal life. In order to keep his body in fit condition for such a return, the living sup-plied him with bread which he could eat spiritually.

The ancient Grecian cult of the dead likewise called for foods

Many of the forms our loaves of bread take were once symbolic in meaning. Braided breads used to signify an offering of hair; bread formed as wreaths (fig. 2–10) represented eternity. A wheel symbolized the sun.

Fig. 2–11a, b, and c Breads from the 4th
Sardinian Crafts Fair, held in Sassari. *Courtesy
of* Domus *Magazine, Milan, Italy.*

to be set out which, after the departed spirits were fed, were consumed by the living.

Memorial services in the Greek Orthodox Church offer *koliva*, a bread made of boiled wheat mixed with raisins, almonds, sesame seeds, and pomegranate seeds. Wheat symbolizes everlasting life, the raisin and pomegranate seeds, sweetness and plenty. Koliva is blessed by priests and eaten by family members and friends of the deceased at several prescribed intervals and bears the initials of the dead person. Eating the loaf represents a wish of the living for the departed to have a sweet and blissful life in heaven.

Sometimes the dead give gifts, too. All Souls' Day finds Sicilian children scurrying through the house to find hidden treasures and thick white cookies called *ossi di mordi* ("bones of the dead"). Believed to be hidden by dead members of the family, these gifts are rewards for the children's good behavior and rekindle fond memories.

England once baked soul cakes in memory of her departed. Children in some villages went "souling" through the streets, crying for soul cakes.

Every year eager boys hungrily scale sixty-foot tall "bun mountains" studded with 30,000 sweet rolls on Cheung Chau Island near Hong Kong. Capturing the highest bun climaxes a celebration in which apologies are offered to the animals and fish killed that year for food. Hungry spirits are invited to join the festivities and partake of the delectable bounty.

Nowhere, though, have the dead been remembered with more celebration, preparation, and humor than in Mexico on November first and second. All Saints' Day and All Souls' Day

Danish Christmas bread saved and nibbled on Easter was once hoped to provide protection against the dangers of snakebite, disease, and other common calamities of the day.

Fig. 2–12 Mrs. Bertha Cracchiolo continues a Sicilian family tradition. A hen formed of flour and water paste is shaped over an egg colored with a dye made by boiling red onion skins. When the hen is put into the oven to bake, the children are told to listen quietly for the "peeping of a chick," the small sound that indicates the egg is done.

comprise a festival of significant proportions in that country. Death, called up by the celebration of the Day of the Faithful Dead, grins satanically from tinsel-eyed sugar skulls (see color section) waiting in rows on candy-store shelves and calls grimly from circular *pan de muerto* ("bread for the dead"), ornamented to represent skull and crossbones. It can be found in bread images of the dead (fig. 2–13), some of them elaborately garmented and often enormous in size, and in whimsical animal forms such as the armadillo (fig. 2–14), llama, and dove.

On All Saints' Day, families in rural areas carry foods, favorites of the deceased in life, to cemeteries and arrange them lovingly on the graves. Adult souls come all through the night as the families wait and watch over them. Angelitos, little angels, come in early afternoon to sample the remembrances brought in their honor. Marigold petals may be strewn from the cemetery to the home of the little spirit so it will not lose its way. Many of the graves are blanketed in yucca blossoms, the flower of the dead. One tiny island village celebrates All Souls' Day with a candlelight procession to the cemetery at midnight. Women and children parade, carrying an arch adorned with flowers and breads baked in animal forms.

In less isolated villages, extravagant food offerings are ar-

Fig. 2–13 Mexican bread for the dead in the shape of a doll, baked for All Souls' Day.

Fig. 2–14 Armadillo, a traditional Mexican "bread for the dead" figure.

ranged on decorated offering tables and placed near the window to be seen by all who pass. The souls for whom offerings are made will be happy to be remembered. Forgotten souls will weep and grieve.

Sourdough

One wonders how many batches of dough were set aside to sour in Egyptian kitchens before someone suggested saving a bit of the old batch to add to the new. The result was instant fermentation, and the beginning of an unforgettable breadmaking technique as appreciated today as then.

Sourdough is a fermented mixture of flour, sugar, and water. A bit of each batch of dough, called the starter, is withheld in the crock to ferment the next batch. In the Russian state of Georgia, a mother gives her newly married daughter a crock of sourdough starter to take to her new home. She uses half in her first loaf of bread and saves the rest in the crock to be "fed" with flour and water for subsequent batches. Sourdough is believed to have come to America in the hold of Christopher Columbus's ship and soon became a staple. Pioneers guarded their sourdough crocks with a dedication and a vehemence. Since the combining of basic ingredients was tricky and the results unpredictable, a starter was a staple worth walking or riding miles to get. Better to keep a source going than to try to start one from scratch. Alaskan prospectors strapped their crocks to their packs so they could have a batch of pancakes or biscuits wherever the campfire was built for the night.

Today San Francisco is generally thought to be the sourdough

Leavening lightens the dough or batter. Coming from a Latin word meaning "to rise," leavening can be accomplished in a variety of ways. Fermentation was the earliest form. Egyptians added beer and grape juice foam to their dough to release the gases (carbon dioxide, air, and water vapor) within and give the loaf greater volume and porosity. A sour piece of dough added to a new batch will do the same thing. Yeast, baking soda, baking powder, and eggs are the most common leavening agents in today's kitchen.

Several centuries before baking powder appeared, salt of hartshorn, made by scraping the antlers of a male deer, was used as a leavening in cookies and breads in the Scandinavian countries. Colonial women leavened cookies with hard wood ash.

Fig. 2–15 Sourdough crab.

capital, and bakers there guard their special starters, some many years old, like ancient treasures. Made commercially with a hard wheat flour, the loaves are baked to tangy perfection in special humidity-controlled ovens that produce a loaf porous and light in the center, chewy brown outside.

San Francisco's own sourdough never wore a more delicious disguise than when sculpted into edible salmons and crabs in commemoration of the 1973 Cable Car Centennial. The crab (fig. 2–15) was shaped in sourdough and textured with a pincer-like tool; the crab's legs were snipped with scissors during baking when they tried to "grow" together. Freshly cooked crab and shrimp filled a hollowed-out cavern in the sourdough crab, while the salmon appeared at buffet fully clothed in apples, grapes, peaches, and a family of soft-ripening cheeses such as Brie and Camembert.

Mexican Bread

The essence of the Mexican spirit is to be found in their vast array of breads. Every aspect of life is depicted in bread, from the objects with which they live, to the whimsical interpretation of the human character, to deeply reverent religious images. Lambs, plump with curly wool; a bride with flowing skirt and powdery veil; nuns and butterflies; the sigh, a roll soft and delicate enough to vanish at a touch; the kiss, two cookies sweetly welded with jam; the shell, which becomes dirty face when dusted with chocolate sugar instead of white; haughty females, shrimps and snails, illusions turning to powder unless handled

Benne cakes originated when African slaves brought benne (sesame) seeds to the South as good luck symbols. They were planted as borders around the cotton fields.

Fig. 2–16 Carved stamps, such as these Indian ones used for printing fabric, can also be used to pattern dough.

delicately; gossip, a long, wicked tongue; harps, spurs, and the rimmed eye of his Satanic majesty—all are to be found in the Mexican *panderia* and mirror the culture as vibrantly and perceptively as do its literature and art.

Chapter 3

Sweets

Fig. 3–1 Fortune cookies.

Honey gathered from hives of wild bees in rocks, crevices, and trees sweetened breads until tame bees became a part of every castle, monastery, or family garden.

Cookie baking has been filling kitchens with fragrance since the days of ancient Egypt when animal- and human-shaped cookies were first formed. Cookies with designs contemporary by today's standards have been recovered from sand-buried outposts in Chinese Turkestan.

Medieval honeycakes were the pride of the bakers' guilds. In these picture cookies could be read the cultural history of much of Europe. Using a honey-flour mixture that took a crisp, clear impression when forced into intricately carved molds, bakers created cookies that were the first pictoral art to circulate among the common man. Embossed with riddles, local customs, biblical parables, and commemorations of special persons and events, these honey-sweetened bits of history were preserved and displayed as edible art.

Lebkuchen, a spice cake made with honey, is a centuries-old festive cake still baked in many countries. This traditional honeycake is believed to have appeared early in history in the Black Forest region of Germany and has frequently been used in the ornate cookie molds of Europe. *Springerle* are hard anise-flavored German cookies, perhaps first cousin to Lebkuchen. Wooden rolling pins and boards carved with birds, fish, flowers, and fruit, are used to emboss the dough, which is then cut into the square sections indicated in the design (fig. 3–2). Left out to dry overnight, the dough is baked next day on an anise-sprinkled cookie sheet. Springerle molds were often enormous in size and depicted horsemen, crinolined ladies, and soldiers. The baked cookies were sometimes delicately painted or tinted.

28

Fig. 3–2 Rolling out springerle dough. Springerle, anise cookies so hard they must be left out overnight to soften for munching, has long been a German Christmas favorite.

Derived from a Dutch word, cookie means "small cake." ("Cookie" is an American usage; they are known in Europe as biscuits.) The Dutch who settled in New York baked *koekjes* in molds that produced embossed designs of eagles or names of illustrious American characters such as Washington or Rip Van Winkle.

Cookies continue to be of deep cultural significance. The baking of traditional favorites or the creation of new ones add meaning and continuity to the festivities which they commemorate.

LEBKUCHEN HEARTS

Itinerant bakers today still follow the fairs of Europe to offer up delicate communications in the form of heart-shaped honeycakes embellished with souvenir pictures and mirrors. Edibly embroidered, these valentines for friends and lovers carry the wishes and desires of the heart. Any time of year might be the right time to bestow upon a beloved friend a beribboned *Mein Schatz* ("my sweetheart") or *Alte Liebe* ("old love") cookie (fig. 3–3). The following recipe makes 8 hearts, about 7″ tall.

Fig. 3–3 Frosted
Lebkuchen heart bearing
sugar-piped message,
meaning "My sweetheart."

Recipe

¾ cup honey	1 teaspoon cinnamon
⅔ cup firmly packed brown sugar	½ teaspoon nutmeg
1 teaspoon grated lemon peel	½ cup minced candied orange peel
¼ cup butter	1 egg yolk, beaten with 1 tablespoon water
2 eggs	1½ cups powdered sugar icing (any recipe), tinted red
½ teaspoon soda	Decorator tubes of frosting (purchased): white, yellow, green
¼ teaspoon salt	Heavy paper for pattern
3¾ cups unsifted flour	
½ cup almonds, ground (optional)	
1 teaspoon ginger	

Combine honey, brown sugar, lemon peel, and butter in a small saucepan. Heat and stir this mixture until the butter melts. Let cool to lukewarm. Beat the eggs until they are foamy and add the honey mixture to them. Stir the soda, salt, flour, ground almonds, ginger, cinnamon, nutmeg, and orange peel until blended and mix them thoroughly into the egg mixture. Cover the dough and chill. Before shaping, allow it to return to room temperature. This dough can be made several days in advance and stored in the refrigerator.

Using heavy paper, cut a heart-shaped pattern approximately 7″ tall. Divide the dough into eight equal parts. Roll one of the portions out on a piece of lightly floured foil. Lay the paper pattern on it and cut around it with a paring knife (fig. 3–4).

Fig. 3–4 A paper pattern is placed on the dough and cut around with a kitchen knife.

Fig. 3–5 Commercial tube frosting being squeezed onto the frosted cookie.

Lift the foil onto a baking sheet. Repeat this same process for each cookie, spacing them slightly apart on the baking sheet. Brush the surfaces of the hearts with the egg-yolk-and-water mixture. Bake the cookies at 350° for 10 to 15 minutes or until they are lightly browned. Cool them completely on a wire rack.

Frost each cookie with the red-tinted powdered sugar icing and decorate with purchased tube frostings (fig. 3–5).

SPECULAAS

Speculaas means "mirror image," which describes the images these cookies are of their charming molds (fig. 3–6). Many European countries have embraced speculaas and varied its spelling and ingredients. A rich dough flavored with brown sugar, cinnamon, and cloves or cardamom, it is a treat not often missing from German Christmas celebrations. It is pressed onto a flat, floured board carved with flowers, birds, and Christmas symbols. A wire, held on the board, is drawn through the dough, leaving only what is in the carved recesses. The board is knocked against a cookie sheet so the quaint little figures tumble out for baking. The recipe below makes about two dozen speculaas.

Spritz are German Christmas cookies whose name means "squirt." German bakers force a rich buttery dough through a meat grinder which has been fitted with a special attachment. The pale dough comes out as a long coil, frequently star-shaped, to be sliced and lightly baked.

Recipe

⅔ cup butter
1 cup flour
1 egg
½ cup brown sugar

1 teaspoon cinnamon
⅛ teaspoon cloves or ¹/₁₆ teaspoon cardamon, crushed

Fig. 3–6 The *kobold* is a favorite motif of German cookie molds. This mischievous little household familiar lives underground and is blamed for minor domestic mishaps.

Work the butter and flour together with a fork until crumbly. Cream the egg and brown sugar and mix in the cinnamon and cloves or cardamom. Combine the egg and butter mixtures well. Spread the dough on a baking sheet and let it chill for 12 hours. Stamp it with molds or press it on a speculaas board. Hold a wire in your hands and draw it across the board leaving only the dough that is in the recesses. Knock the board on a cookie sheet to dislodge the molded dough. Roll out the remaining dough and repeat the procedure. Bake for 10 minutes at 350°.

Scones, light and feathery, stuffed with currants or not, are the hot bread of Scotland. Tradition has it the name came from a parish in Perthshire which was the site of the Stone of Destiny, or Scone, upon which the kings of Scotland were crowned.

SHORTBREAD SPOOL COOKIES

Scotch shortbread, pale and rich, is baked at a low temperature and holds its shape well. It is easily molded either by pressing a cookie stamp down on it or by filling a carved mold with dough and turning the dough out onto a cookie sheet. A favorite motif of shortbread molds is the Scotch thistle (fig. 3–7). Cookies may also be shaped without using a standard mold. Good designs are to be found in surprising places. Gears from a meat grinder and the end of a plastic thread spool (fig. 3–8) are examples. The recipe below makes approximately three dozen cookies.

Recipe

1½ cups butter	2 cups flour
1 cup cornstarch	¼ teaspoon salt
1 cup confectioner's sugar	½ teaspoon vanilla

Cream the butter in a large mixing bowl. Mix the cornstarch, confectioner's sugar, flour, and salt together. Add the flour mix-

Fig. 3–7 Shortbread imprinted with a wooden mold. Thistles are often incorporated into the designs of Scotch cookie molds.

Fig. 3–8 Shortbread cookies stamped with a thread spool.

ture to the butter and mix until a soft dough is formed. Add vanilla and blend well. Shape into balls the size of a small walnut and place on an ungreased cookie sheet, about ½" apart. Dip the end of a thread spool (or other patterned implement) into flour and press it down onto the ball of dough to imprint a design. Lift the spool carefully from the dough and repeat this process with the other balls of dough. Bake the cookies at 350° for 15 minutes or until the edges are delicately browned.

GINGERBREAD

Whether cut into rows of plump, molassesy men, shaped in intricately carved fruitwood molds, or used as the "lumber and stone" of castles and cottages, gingerbread is both food and art and has been around for hundreds, perhaps thousands, of years. Wealthy Grecians of 2800 BC flocked to the Isle of Rhodes to enjoy an early honey-and-cinnamon-sweetened version of this delicacy.

Medieval ladies gifted their favorite knights with gingerbread morsels resembling embossed leather, often gold leafed and shaped as a fleur-de-lis. Guinevere might have bestowed just such an edible token of affection and admiration on Sir Lancelot as he emerged victorious from tournament battle.

Fragrantly spicy breezes wafted from gingerbread stalls at the great fairs of the Middle Ages, tempting fairgoers to select from an array of dark cakes, fancifully painted with colored sugars and gilded.

Elaborately carved, often larger than life, wooden ginger-

Fig. 3–9 Twin-figured
gingerbread from medieval
mold design.

bread molds froze in history images of elegantly attired and
coifed aristocrats as well as cherubs, roosters, saints, mermaids,
and symbolic scenes (figs. 3–9 and 3–10). The ever-familiar
heart was originally a talisman against evil and later came to

*In the Netherlands, St. Nicholas
has long been remembered and
commemorated in gingerbread.
A third-century bishop, St.
Nicholas provided dowries for
girls without means and became
the patron saint of marriageable
young men and women.*

Fig. 3–10 Gingerbread
mermaid. Medieval design.

express love. Babies and rabbits represented fertility; dogs, fidelity; and a stag, virility. St. George and the Dragon, symbols of the struggle between good and evil, have often been represented in gingerbread.

The carvers of these molds had their own guild, as did the gingerbread makers themselves. Many European countries baked this malleable bread for festive occasions, and, it would seem, for art itself. Though the original gingerbread cakes went the way of all sweets, the molds from which they came may still be seen in the fine museums of the world.

The colonists did not leave behind their treasured molds or recipes when they set out for the crossing, and gingerbread wasn't long in capturing a niche in the baking traditions of America. George Washington's mother made and served the heavily spiced molasses cake to illustrious guests. John Adams once said, in reference to the Molasses Act passed by the British Parliament in 1633, that molasses was an essential ingredient in the American Revolution, molasses and ginger being so vitally linked with American cooking.

"Muster Day Gingerbread" commemorated a New England pre–Civil War tradition that required all men ages 18–45 to show up for training the first Tuesday of every June. Beginning at nine o'clock in the morning, the training day became a traditional party with the men bringing all available relatives—wives, sisters, cousins, grandmothers, and the rest. Such a fine occasion demanded gingerbread, of course, and vendors sold hot, glazed slabs for a penny apiece.

Fig. 3–11 Gingerbread log cabin. *Baked by Bonna and Hal Nelson.*

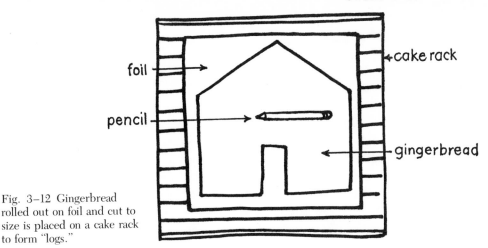

Fig. 3–12 Gingerbread
rolled out on foil and cut to
size is placed on a cake rack
to form "logs."

Hardly a family kitchen since has been without the occasional fragrance and anticipation of an oven-load of ginger-spicy cookies to treasure only as long as it takes to eat them up.

This gingerbread log cabin (fig. 3–11), shake-roofed and chinked with white frosting, was baked and "raised" by Bonna and Hal Nelson.

To form the logs on the cabin, Mrs. Nelson rolled out gingerbread cookie dough ¼" thick (use your own favorite recipe, or follow the one on page 40) on a piece of aluminum foil. Using a paper pattern, she cut a wall section. The foil was then lifted onto a cake rack. An unsharpened pencil was used to press the dough between the wires giving it a corrugated look (figs. 3–12 and 3–13). Each section was baked right on the rack and thoroughly cooled before it was removed. The sections were

Fig. 3–13 Corrugated side
sections of cabin, made by pressing the
dough between the wires of the cake rack.

dried 3 or 4 days before being assembled with powdered sugar frosting.

STAINED-GLASS COOKIES

Ilse Johnson, an artist and crafts designer, is the inventor of the "stained-glass" cookie. Ilse relishes the challenge of solving problems visually whatever the medium, cookies and clay being two of her favorites. (Her husband designed the cookie snail, fig. 3–14. Others of her design are shown in the color section.) An associate professor of art at Trenton State College, Ilse was a guiding force and a participant in a major show featuring baking as art at the Museum of Contemporary Crafts in New York City.

Fig. 3–14 Phillip Johnson's cookie snail. A designer of children's toys, Mr. Johnson is also producer and co-editor of a juvenile magazine. *Photo courtesy of Ilse Johnson.*

General directions

Select your design and draw it on paper. You may be inspired by one in this book (see color section or the "Stained Glass Cookie Cat" project) or make up one completely your own. Remember that it is easiest to work with a design in which the entire outside outline of your stained-glass cookie is made of dough. Each color section must be surrounded by dough, to contain the melted candy.

Make up a batch of cookie dough. Gingerbread (recipe appears on page 40) is an excellent dough to work with, but you could try using any firm, easy-to-handle cookie dough.

Impress the outlines of your design on aluminum foil by placing the pattern over the foil and tracing over the design with a blunt pencil. Roll the cookie dough into ropes and arrange the ropes on the foil, fitting them to your outline. To straighten lines and correct mistakes, use a toothpick dipped in flour. Press dough together with the toothpick at points where lines meet or cross. A firm smooth outline is required to hold candy inside the pattern. Use the toothpick to make a hole in the top of the cookie for hanging. Make the hole large enough to accommodate expanding of dough during baking.

Lift the foil and cookie design onto a baking sheet and bake according to the cookie recipe directions.

When the cookie is done baking, fill in the spaces of your cookie design with candy, using purchased hard candy or home-made candy (recipe appears on page 41). Crush the candy with a mallet or meat tenderizer, and sprinkle bits and chunks of it in the areas you want to fill with color. Place the candy-filled designs in a 275° oven for about 2 minutes. The candy will melt very quickly and will brown if left in too long. Test the candy by touching it with a toothpick. As soon as it is soft, the design is finished. If the candy does not completely fill the cookie shape, sprinkle in a bit more and put it back in the oven for another minute or two.

When the designs are completely cool, peel the foil off the back and hang the cookies with nylon filament. Store them in a cool place but not in the refrigerator. If hung, protect the floor under them because the candy may weep.

Barbrack, a fortune-telling fruit loaf, is baked for Irish Halloween festivities. Tokens hidden inside the sweet and sticky-crusted loaf tell the fortunes of those who eat it. A ring signifies marriage; a silver coin, wealth; and a button, blessedness.

Another effective technique to use in the creation of stained-glass cookies is, instead of outlining the design with thin coils of dough, to roll the dough out thin and cut out a design, lifting the dough out of the sections that are to be filled in with candy. (This technique is used in the "Stained-Glass Cookie Cat" project.) Cookie cutters may be used to cut out the design, or you may use a pattern of your own making.

When the basic outline has been defined, press a hole in the top of the cookie with a chopstick or toothpick. Make all openings larger than seems necessary to accommodate shrinkage during baking.

Texture the cookie dough before baking, using instruments to impress interesting patterns in the dough. Ordinary kitchen utensils (potato peeler, garlic press, pastry blender, spoon handles) can be used to create very attractive designs.

Dick Crispo, a multi-media artist, baked some striking abstract stained glass cookies using this cut-out technique (see color section). An ordained priest in the Church of Antioch, Dick is an authority on folk art and the founder of a program that takes art to the people, called Museum on Wheels. Examples of his work are found in museums and private collections in many countries.

STAINED-GLASS COOKIE CAT

To create this self-satisfied—and entirely edible—cat in his candy and gingerbread frame (fig. 3–15), first collect all the ma-

Fig. 3–15 Stained-glass cookie cat. The cookie frame is filled with crushed candy.

terials and have them at hand, and make up batches of the gingerbread dough and lollipop candy (recipes below). If you don't want to make the candy yourself, buy colored candies. However, most store-bought candies tend to lose some color when baked. The lollipop recipe given below makes a vibrantly colored candy. Step-by-step instructions for making the cookie cat appear after the recipes.

Materials

1 batch gingerbread cookie dough (recipe follows)
1 batch lollipop candy (recipe follows)
lightweight paper
aluminum foil

cookie sheet
skewer or toothpick
meat tenderizer or mallet
kitchen knife
dinner-sized plate
salad-sized plate

Edible Gingerbread Dough

2½ cups all-purpose flour
1 teaspoon cinnamon
1 teaspoon nutmeg
1 tablespoon ginger
¼ teaspoon salt
¼ cup granulated sugar

⅓ cup dark molasses
⅓ cup packed brown sugar
½ cup butter
½ teaspoon baking soda
1 egg

Sift the flour, spices, salt, and granulated sugar together into a bowl. Heat the molasses to the boiling point and remove it from the heat. Add the brown sugar and butter to the molasses and stir until the butter melts. Add baking soda and stir well. Pour it over the flour-spice mixture, mixing well. Add the egg and knead until the dough holds together. Chill it while making the candy.

Lollipop Candy

2 cups sugar	½ cup water
1 cup light corn syrup	food coloring: 2 colors

Mix the sugar, corn syrup, and water together in a medium-size saucepan. Stir to blend well and cook over high heat to 300° on a candy thermometer (hard crack stage). Remove at once from the heat.

If you do not have a candy thermometer, you can use the water method to check for the hard crack stage. Drop a small quantity of the syrup into ice water. If the syrup separates into threads that are hard and brittle, the candy is done.

Have a small pan and spoon ready for each of the two colors you plan to use. Pour some of the syrup into a pan and add food coloring drop by drop. Stir the mixture as little as possible to avoid trapping air bubbles and causing the candy to lose its translucent quality.

Because the candy hardens as it cools, you will need to reheat the syrup occasionally over moderate heat. Pour the syrup into small puddles on foil to allow them to dry thoughly.

Cookie Construction

1. Trace the cat pattern (fig. 3–16) on lightweight paper. Cut it out and put it aside.

2. Using a floured rolling pin, roll out the chilled cookie dough on a large piece of foil. The dough should be quite thin to minimize puffing in the oven.

3. Invert a dinner plate on the rolled dough and cut around it with a kitchen knife. Remove the plate and center an inverted salad plate on the remaining dough. Cut around this also. Remove the plate.

4. Lift the foil with the cookie on it to a cookie sheet. The cookie sheet should be sturdy and quite level to avoid distortion of the design while the cookie bakes.

5. Place the cat and fish patterns on the cookie and cut around them. Remove all the excess dough (fig. 3–17).

6. Roll a small ball of dough in your hand to form the cat's face. Pat it into place. Three tiny balls of dough form the cat's eyes and nose.

Fig. 3–16 Pattern for cookie cat.

7. Press whiskers, mouth, and eyelashes into the face with a bamboo skewer or toothpick. Press in the other design details on the cat and fish at this time.

8. Imprint the frame of the cookie with the end of a kitchen knife or another object that yields a similar pattern (fig. 3–18).

9. Cut a rectangle of dough the width of the cookie frame and imprint the words "Yum-Yum" with the skewer. Trim the rectangle lengthwise and place it on the bottom of the cookie, following the curve of the frame. Texture the edges with a skewer.

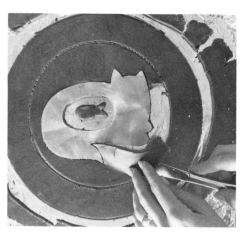

Fig. 3–17 Excess dough is lifted away from the design.

Fig. 3–18 The end of a knife is used to texture the outer edge of the cookie.

10. Place the cookie in a 350° oven for 10 minutes or until a test cookie is just done.

11. While the cookie is baking, crush several chunks of candy with a meat tenderizer or mallet.

Fig. 3–19 Crushed candy is sprinkled into the cookie frame.

12. Remove the cookie from the oven and fill the open areas with crushed candy (fig. 3–19). The candy will spread as it melts so it is not necessary to completely fill the open areas. More candy may be added later if needed.

15. Return the cookie to the 350° oven and allow the candy to melt. It only takes a couple of minutes, depending on how finely crushed the candy is. When the candy is smoothly melted, take the cookie from the oven. Allow it to cool completely before removing it from the foil.

HOMEMADE COOKIE MOLDS

If you can't find the right mold for cookies or a dough project, you can always make exactly what you want. Using a modeling compound that bakes hard in the oven, you can either imprint a design or scoop it out. Craft shops and art supply stores carry various brands of compound and each is made up in a slightly different way. Be sure to buy a brand that can be used in contact with food. Follow the manufacturer's directions.

Generally speaking, you work a piece of the modeling compound until it is smooth and pliable. Roll it to about ½" thick. If you are making a cookie mold, keep in mind the size of the finished cookie. A 5" square would probably be the biggest cookie you could make that wouldn't crumble; 3" to 4" would be a better size.

Make a design on the flattened dough by impressing a piece of costume jewelry (fig. 3–20) or scraping out a pattern with a

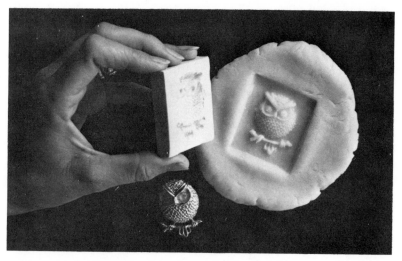

Fig. 3–20 Commercial modeling compounds may be imprinted to form cookie molds. *Courtesy of Hazel Tripp.*

knife or spoon handle. Texture may be added with any implement you have handy. Keep in mind as you make each mold that the finished project will be a mirror image. Reverse any words you might use. Trim the mold to the shape you want.

Dry the cookie molds according to the instructions on the package. When they are hard, you can do a little additional work on your design to be sure there are no undercuts (depressions that turn in instead of straight up) to spoil the impression on the cookie.

Make the shortbread cookie dough in this book (page 33). Use it at room temperature and handle the molds carefully. Before you begin to stamp cookies, press the dough lightly against the molds and the flour them. You will have to reflour the mold before each impression. Bake the cookies as directed.

Syrian bread stamps embossed with delicate flower and bird designs are customarily used to imprint wafers for religious ceremonies.

MARZIPAN

Marzipan appears to be almost ageless. Shrewsbury Simnel, a cake topped with twelve marzipan balls, celebrated the ancient Roman feast of Matronila honoring Juno, the protectress of home. For this one day a year, Roman wives entertained their slaves and were presented with gifts by their husbands in honor of the occasion.

Sweet delight of Persian princes, marzipan arrived in Medieval Europe in the duffle of returning Crusaders. Shaped like a coin and called by an Arabic name, "marchpane" was adopted by many European cities. Master bakers sculpted and molded the almond-paste confectionery into works of art. These delightful novelties were traded all over Europe and took their place in the culinary customs of many countries.

Marzipan pigs, plump and pink, appear faithfully as good luck prizes in Scandinavian Christmases; and miniature replicas of fruit (fig. 3–21), vegetables, and holiday tokens once held a place of enchantment in America's own holiday festivities.

Miniature roosters, ivory pale pigs with red tails, serpents twisting up through roundelays of frogs, corn on the cob, bescaled salmon, and figs all swirl deliciously through the celebrations of Spain and Portugal. Three-headed marzipan monsters join oven-browned dragons piped with sugar flourishes in adding friendly fright to the holiday melee.

Here are two recipes for marzipan, one starting from scratch and one using a canned almond paste base. Each may be tinted by kneading in the food coloring or brushing it on. Flavorings such as vanilla or a variety of liqueurs may also be added.

In Latin America squash seeds are washed and ground and sweetened. As this mixture begins to harden, little candy ducks, chickens, and fanciful shapes are molded and decorated by hand, sweets and trinkets in one.

Fig. 3–21 Marzipan apples, 1½" high. Cloves form the stems.

Traditional Marzipan

2 cups blanched almonds	4 cups confectioner's sugar
2 teaspoons almond extract	4 egg whites, slightly beaten

Grind the almonds in an electric blender or grind them 4 times in an electric nut blender. They must be extremely fine. Combine the ground almonds, almond extract, and confectioner's sugar. Add the egg whites to this mixture, one teaspoon at a time, beating vigorously with a spoon. Continue adding egg whites until the mixture looks moist. Knead the mixture with your hands until it is smooth and pliable. You may need to dust your hands with confectioner's sugar to do the kneading. If the mixture becomes too thick, work in a little lemon juice drop by drop. If it becomes too oily, work it in a dish of ice. After it is kneaded, mold it into the desired shape. Refer to the directions below for flavoring, coloring, and shaping. This recipe makes approximately 3 cups of marzipan.

Quick Marzipan

If you prefer not to start from scratch, try this recipe. It begins with the canned almond paste available in most grocery stores and gourmet food shops.

1 cup almond paste
½ cup soft butter
3 cups confectioner's sugar

Beat the almond paste, butter, and sugar until smooth. Refer to the directions below for flavoring, coloring, and shaping. This recipe makes about 2½ cups of marzipan.

Flavoring and Coloring

Marzipan may be flavored deliciously. Before coloring, knead in either vanilla or a liqueur such as rum, brandy, cointreau, kirsch, or Kahlua. Use 1 teaspoon of flavoring for every cup of marzipan. If you are planning to tint the marzipan, be careful not to add a flavoring that will color the dough.

Marzipan can be tinted by kneading in food coloring or brushing it on with a soft brush after the shapes have been molded. The directions that follow use regular food colorings. More vibrant colors can be obtained with the food colorings used by bakers. These are available at most large department stores or bakery supply houses and are in paste form. They are more expensive but a little goes a long way and the range of colors is exciting.

Orange dough: Use 3 drops of red food coloring to 2 drops of yellow.

Green dough: Tint to a desired shade with the green food coloring or use a few drops of yellow and a drop of blue.

Yellow dough: Use the amount of yellow food coloring required to give the color intensity you want.

Red dough: Use the amount of red food coloring required to give the intensity of color you want.

Shaping

Marzipan can be molded into fancy shapes using the tiny molds available at kitchen specialty shops or it can be shaped by hand. Small fruit and vegetable shapes are great favorites. Tiny leaves and stems may be formed with the dough itself. Cloves and cinnamon sticks also make good stems and blossom ends.

Apples: Roll red marzipan into a ball. Use a piece of cinnamon stick for the stem and a clove for the blossom end. Brush on a blush using ⅛ teaspoon red food coloring diluted with 1 teaspoon water.

Apricots: Roll a ball out of orange marzipan. Make a crease down the side with a toothpick. Stick a clove in the blossom end and brush on a blush (see apples).

Bananas: Shape yellow marzipan into a fat cigar. Flatten the

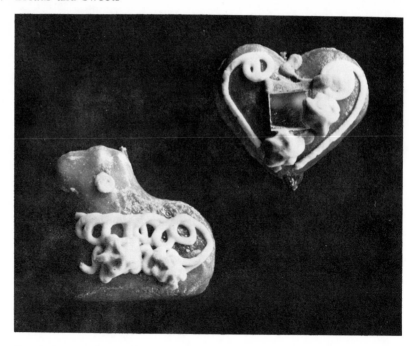

Fig. 3–22 Yugoslavian Christmas tree ornaments. Pairs of tiny cookies are put together back-to-back to give a rounded bell, lamb, or star shape. Decorated with colored frosting and mirrors, they are sprayed with varnish to last for years. *Courtesy of Regina Moritz.*

sides slightly to show the planes of the fruit and curve it slightly. Brush on the dark markings, using 3 drops of red, 2 drops of yellow, and 1 drop of blue diluted in ½ teaspoon of water.

Carrots: Form a cone-shaped piece out of orange marzipan. Run a bit of green dough through a garlic press for the carrot tops and texture the carrot with a toothpick.

Oranges: Form a round ball out of orange marzipan. Use a bit of green dough for the blossom end. Texture the skin of the orange with a blunt toothpick.

Pears: Roll yellow marzipan into a ball and elongate it to a cone shape. Use a cinnamon stick for the stem and brush a red blush on the pear cheeks (see apples).

Peas: Form green dough into a ball and flatten it into a circle. Shape five or six tiny balls to lay down the center of the flattened circle. Pinch the ends of the pod up around the peas.

Strawberries: Form a ball out of red marzipan and elongate it into a strawberry shape. Texture the strawberry with a toothpick and use a bit of green marzipan for a stem and leaves.

Turnips: Form a fat cone out of untinted marzipan. Make the leafy top by pressing green dough through a garlic press. Brush on a purplish blush, using 4 drops of red and 2 drops of blue diluted with a little water.

Roosters: Roll untinted marzipan into a ball and shape a rooster body. Add a red comb and wattles and red and green tail feathers. Use a tiny ball of natural dough with an even tinier ball of dark dough patted on for the eyes. You could paint the center of the eye using the color mixed for the banana markings.

PAINTED COOKIES

A smooth white frosting centered with a spray of flowers decorates heart-shaped butter cookies for valentine giving (fig. 3–23). Keep the painted flowers very light and delicate for the most appetite appeal. Bake your favorite cookies and use this white frosting to spread over them, adding a few drops of water if needed to keep it from showing any lines from the knife.

When the frosting has set, use a small watercolor brush and a mixture of egg yolk and food coloring to paint the roses.

Cookie Frosting

    2 egg whites
    1 pound confectioner's sugar
    ½ teaspoon vanilla

Beat the egg whites in a medium-sized bowl till soft peaks form. Beat in the confectioner's sugar and vanilla. Add water, one

One of Mexico's most important festive breads is the rosca de San Isidro *("ring of Saint Isidore"), the Plowman. Large and white, this circular loaf celebrates May 15, Saint Isidore's day. The oxen in the fields wear flowered garlands around their necks and the plows are decorated to commemorate the saint who protects the crops. When Saint Isidore goes to Mass, an angel guards his plow.*

Fig. 3–23 Frosted cookies painted with a mixture of egg yolk and food coloring.

teaspoon at a time, until the frosting will spread smoothly leaving no marks from the knife.

PAINTED PIES

Krapfen, a light feathery donut, was a Viennese matrimonial trap. During Fasching, a celebration beginning the day after Epiphany and lasting until Shrove Tuesday, a young man might become obligated to marriage if a girl chose to break her krapfen for him. A broken krapfen was a token of engagement.

At a time when giant plastic hamburgers qualified as art, Jim Fobel and Jim Boleach, both of New York, carried the food art concept a step further by creating art on food, real food. Pies painted with everything from patchwork to bluejeans and bandanas led to a whole line of stenciled foods. Their portrait pies, bearing painted likenesses of some of the country's most illustrious film and news people, have appeared at many celebrity gatherings.

Jim and Jim, who spearhead their own company, design for top magazine publications and have recently authored a book on stenciling.

For a very special occasion even a pie might be improved with some adornment. Color as edible as the pie itself bakes into a rich glaze as the pastry browns (fig. 3–24 and color section). Begin with a simple design to become familiar with the technique. Then try something that involves modeling with darks and lights. You can achieve a three-dimensional look by using full strength food coloring for dark areas or areas of greater color intensity.

Fig. 3–24 Holiday pie brightly decorated with egg yolk and food coloring "paints." (See also color section.) *Jim Fobel and Jim Boleach.*

Materials

pastry for a two-crust pie
pie filling (choose one that does not tend to boil over)
pie tin
baking sheet
waxed paper
aluminum foil
plastic wrap

1 egg yolk
1 egg
1 cup water
food coloring: red, yellow, and blue
small watercolor brush
toothpick

Instructions

1. Prepare the pie crust. Divide the dough in half and roll each portion out on waxed paper. Trim the edges to form two 11″ circles. Cover both circles with plastic wrap and refrigerate. Chill the pastry scraps as well for use in testing colors.

2. Mix one egg yolk and one teaspoon of water in a cup. Using a sheet of aluminum foil as your palette, stir a little of the egg yolk mixture into a drop of blue food coloring with a toothpick.

3. Mix the red and green colorings in the same way, spacing the pools of color on the foil so they will not run together.

4. Remove one of the pastry circles from the refrigerator. Lift the waxed paper and pastry onto a baking sheet, for ease of handling. Using the watercolor brush, carefully paint your design onto the pastry, making sure to coat each color area well and to clean the brush between applications of different colors.

5. When the design is completed, again refrigerate the pastry (leave it on the baking sheet). Do not cover it this time or the colors may smear. Cover the egg paints for use in later retouching.

6. Remove the undecorated pastry round from the refrigerator. Prepare the pie filling. Fit the lower crust into the pie tin and fill it.

7. Remove the painted pastry from the refrigerator, let it return to room temperature, and then carefully fit it onto the top of the pie. Crimp the edges. Cut four ½″ slits in the top crust near the border.

8. Bake at 425° for 15 minutes. Then brush the crimped edges with a mixture of one egg and 2 teaspoons water. Recoat with the egg mixture after another 10 minutes of baking. Bake 5 more minutes and remove from the oven to cool. Retouch any part of the design that may have cracked or separated during baking.

Part II

CRAFT DOUGHS

Chapter 4

Fig. 4–1 Incised baker's clay medallion by Sharon Spencer.

Baker's Clay

This "fat" inedible dough is very satisfying for sculpting and modeling since it is highly malleable and seldom cracks during drying. It can be molded, snipped, braided, textured, used in dough appliqué, and pressed through a garlic or cookie press.

Experimenting with the length of baking time will achieve a range of shades from ivory to deep brown. Smaller dough pieces may be baked, pressed into damp dough, and baked again, thus multiplying the possibilities for variety in natural coloration. Slight puffing and distortion are the nature and the character of this dough and will offer sometimes unexpected, nearly always interesting, variations to a design plan.

In the Middle East, bread serves as food, fork, and vessel in one. Food is scooped up or spread on dry, flat Arab bread and all is eaten.

Recipe

> 4 cups unsifted flour
> 1 cup salt
> 1½ cups water

Combine all ingredients in a mixing bowl. Turn out on a lightly floured board and knead until smooth, adding a little more water if the dough is too stiff to work. This dough will last indefinitely in the refrigerator. After it has been stored, you will need to add more flour.

Because the dough tends to dry on your hands, it is a convenience to have a dampened washcloth near your work area. This is especially helpful when working with colored dough.

Shape the dough as desired on a foil-covered cookie sheet and bake at 300° until hard. Colors tend to dull when projects are

Fig. 4–2 A variety of objects were used to texture this baker's clay Victorian. Gables, windows, and doors were added to a simply shaped background.

Fig. 4–3 Kay Whitcomb's "Tree of Life." Baker's clay formed over an armature of heavy wire.

Bread basket. Made of baker's clay.

Hen and chick plaque. Made of baker's clay.

Cookie panel, 13″ x 18″, combining gingerbread and vanilla cookie dough, by Ilse Johnson. Cracks and irregularities emphasize the edible look of the panel. *Ilse Johnson*

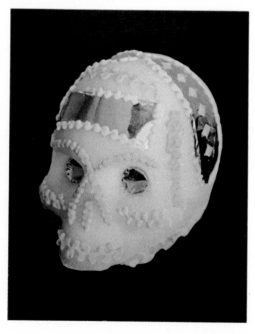

Sugar skull commemorates All Soul's Day in Mexico. *Monterey Peninsula Museum of Art*

"Two on a Horse" by Kay Whitcomb. A baker's clay wall hanging built over a wire armature.

Stained-glass cookie abstracts by Dick Crispo. Made with gingerbread and crushed candy.
Eleanor Melvin

Eagle mask. Made of cornstarch dough.

Hand-rolled beads made of
breadcrumb dough.

Appliqued mirror frame. Made of baker's clay tinted with food coloring.

"Table Set for Four" by Ilse Johnson. Made of gingerbread and vanilla cookie dough, everything is full-scale and entirely edible, even the forks.
Ilse Johnson

Shepherd. Ecuadorian figure
made of bread. *Monterey
Peninsula Museum of Art*

Pie, edibly painted by
Jim Fobel and Jim
Boleach. *Jim Fobel and
Jim Boleach*

Traditional flower-encrusted wedding bread from Crete stands on a Greek market shelf. *Mr. and Mrs. F. E. Rainer*

Nativity by six-year-old child. Made of cornstarch dough painted with a glaze of white glue and food coloring.

Fountain by Ruth Asawa. Sculpted in baker's clay and cast in bronze. *Hyatt on Union Square, San Francisco, California*

Fig. 4–4 "Mother & Child" with mirror, by Kay Whitcomb. Approximately 16″ high, this figure was painted in clear candy colors and brushed with a transluscent blue glaze.

overbaked and underbaked projects don't keep as well. So watch the timing carefully!

Finished pieces are strong and will last indefinitely when painted or sprayed with a protective coating. Spray or brush on clear enamel, acrylic, shellac, or varnish. These finishes usually come in a choice of matte or gloss.

Baker's clay is a medium in which one's imagination can run wild, as Kay Whitcomb's pieces illustrate (figs. 4–3 and 4–4). An artist whose first medium is architectural enameling on steel, Kay energetically applies her creativity to a myriad of other art forms. "Two on a Horse" (see color section) is another example of her whimsical and delighted approach to baker's clay. Grinning, pointy-nosed children sit astride a steed of fine mane and tail, all obviously bound for adventure grown-ups need not even try to imagine.

APPLIQUED MIRROR FRAME

Materials

1 batch of baker's clay
flour
food coloring: red, blue, and yellow
1 small, round, unframed mirror (4½″ to 5″ in diameter)
2 short screws
10″ piece of wire or string
clear acrylic spray

miscellaneous items to use as stamps for pressing designs into mirror frame
kitchen knife
rolling pin
plastic bag
aluminum foil
dinner plate, smooth edged

Instructions

1. Make one batch of baker's clay using the recipe given at the beginning of this chapter.

2. Working on a piece of foil, knead the dough smooth and pat it into a large thick circle. Roll the dough to a round approximately ½" thick.

3. Lay the dinner plate face down on the dough and trim around the plate with a kitchen knife. Lift away the excess dough and keep it in a plastic bag until you are ready to use it. Remove the plate and smooth the edges of the dough carefully.

4. Joining 6" wide strips of aluminum foil by crimping the ends together, make a single strip long enough to encircle the mirror. Crumple it loosely around the mirror's edge. This provides support for the expanding dough and prevents the later cracking of the mirror. (This piece of foil remains in the finished mirror frame.) Center the mirror on the dough. Using equal pressure all around, push the foil-edged mirror about ¼" into the dough, with the mirror facing upward.

5. Pat the dough gently down around the mirror to encase it (fig. 4–5). Cover the frame with a towel to keep it from drying out.

6. Indent a fist-sized piece of the remaining dough with your fingers and squeeze a few drops of red food coloring into the indentation. Knead the color into the dough and continue to add coloring until the desired shade of pink is achieved. If the dough becomes sticky from the addition of liquid food coloring, simply add a bit more flour and work it through. Using this same technique, color half the remaining dough medium blue and the last

Fig. 4–5 Pressing down dough to encase the mirror.

Fig. 4–6 Balls are positioned around mirror's edge and imprinted with a stamp.

of it yellow. Keep these last two balls of dough in the plastic bag.

7. Roll the pink dough into 16 balls, each approximately the size of a small walnut. Position these balls evenly on the dough around the mirror, along the inside edge of the frame. You may need fewer than 16 balls, depending on their size.

8. Look around you for an implement that yields an interesting impression when pressed into dough. The pink balls on the mirror frame pictured (fig. 4–6 and color section) were imprinted with a ceramic cookie press. Sewing machine bobbins, gears from children's toys, old jewelry, and spools all make effective impressions. Try several possibilities on unused pieces of dough to decide which suits the frame best. Dust the stamp with flour, shake off the excess, and press it down onto each pink ball gently but firmly.

9. Roll 16 smaller balls of blue dough and elongate them to about 1½". Position these on the frame. Press the point of a long potato peeler or kitchen knife into the blue dough for an interesting texture (fig. 4–7).

10. Roll the yellow dough into 32 tiny balls and position these (refer to color section, as needed). Press each down with the rounded tip of a ballpoint pen.

11. Texture the outside edge of the mirror frame by pressing short lines all around it with a kitchen knife.

12. Using the edges of the foil on which you are working, lift the mirror frame onto a cookie sheet for baking.

13. To minimize puffing of the dough in the oven, dry the mirror frame very slowly. Preheat the oven to 250°, turn it off, and place the cookie sheet inside. Leave it overnight if possible,

Fig. 4–7 A long-handled vegetable peeler may be used to texture the blue strips.

or until the oven cools. Then turn the oven to 250° and bake the frame for another 2 hours, watching it carefully to see that it doesn't brown.

14. When the frame is dry and cool, it should be sprayed or painted with clear acrylic. Several coats will give gloss and protection from humidity. Shield the mirror while spraying by pressing crumpled aluminum foil over it (fig. 4–8).

15. For hanging, screw 2 short screws into the back side of

Fig. 4–8 Crushed aluminum foil shields the mirror during spraying.

the frame a little above center and a few inches apart. Remove these screws and fill the hole with epoxy or another strong glue. Immediately replace the screws. When the glue has dried, wrap each screw with the end of the wire. Your mirror is now ready for hanging.

BAKER'S BEADS

neat …

Long ago, the word *bidden,* from which comes our word *bead,* meant "to pray." Beads were used as an aid to prayer as the faithful kept count of their repeated devotions to God. The wampum of the American Indian and the trade beads from Africa, on the other hand, are examples of the use of beads as money in primitive societies. In Iran, donkeys wear glazed blue lava beads to deflect the evil eye.

Nearly all cultures have enjoyed beads for the pleasure of ornamentation. They are strung to be worn around the necks of empresses and kindergartners. Bead stitchery has enriched the ceremonial clothing of Chief Joseph of the Nez Percés as well as

string on dental floss

See p. 65 for beads you don't have to roll

Fig. 4–9 Baker's beads, rolled from colored baker's clay.

the inaugural gowns of several first ladies. Beads have been made from seeds, shells, teeth, stone, and pearls. Most are a single strand ornamentation but some are as elaborate as the heavy cloisonné collars worn by Egyptian pharaohs. Hips, ankles, noses, ears, and navels have all been decorated at various times with beads. One ancient people even threaded beads on eyelashes.

Handrolled beads have an appeal that is at once earthy and sophisticated. Baker's clay can be used very effectively to make an infinite variety of interesting beads (fig. 4–9). Breadcrumb dough (chapter 7) is also an excellent medium for beadmaking, and you will find further descriptions for bead projects in that chapter.

The instructions below are for a string of baker's clay beads in shades of red and orange. Any colors may be substituted for the ones used here. Later you will probably want to use any number of color combinations and variations in making necklaces of your own color preference.

One batch of baker's clay will make four or five strings of beads, depending on the length and the size of the beads.

Materials

1 batch of baker's clay	plastic drinking straws
medium-sized needle	single-edged razor blade
waxed or unwaxed dental floss	damp washcloth for wiping
flour	hands
tempera paints, red and	clear acrylic to brush or spray
orange	on
aluminum foil	necklace clasp (optional)
cookie sheet	

Coloring Dough

1. Make one batch of baker's clay using the recipe given at the beginning of this chapter.

2. Divide the dough into three parts. Flatten one portion, and wipe orange tempera paint over its surface. Fold the dough over and knead it until the color is evenly distributed. If the dough becomes sticky from the addition of paint, work in extra flour.

3. Color an equal amount of the dough red, using the same procedure.

Forming Beads

1. You will need about 110 pea-sized beads, about ¼" wide, to make a string of beads 26" long. This length will fit over your head. Anything shorter will need a clasp, which you can buy at a craft supply shop.

2. Using part of the orange dough, form pea-sized beads by rolling a small piece of dough in your hand (fig. 4–10). Place beads on a foil-covered cookie sheet, spacing them so they do not stick to one another.

3. Use part of the red dough to form more beads and add these to the ones on the cookie sheet.

4. Combine a small amount of orange dough with a little of the red, knead together, and form beads of this mixture. Repeat, using more of one color and less of the other. You may also add some uncolored dough to the portions of red and orange doughs to produce pale tints of the red, the orange, or any of the shades between the two colors.

5. Marbeled beads combine well with solid colors and are made by combining pieces of dough of two or three colors and kneading only until an attractive swirling effect is achieved.

6. Fold the edges of the foil sheet up to prevent the dried beads from rolling off into the oven. Bake the beads at 325° for about 5 minutes, or until the outside is hard but the center is still soft. Test by pinching gently.

7. Remove the beads from the oven and let them cool.

An English lass selling buns on the streets of Bath cried "Solet Lune" ("sun and moon") to attract customers in 1770. From the French words soleil *and* lune, *the name was an apt discription of her golden-topped, white-bottomed rolls. The Americanized "Sally Lunn" is now more of a bread.*

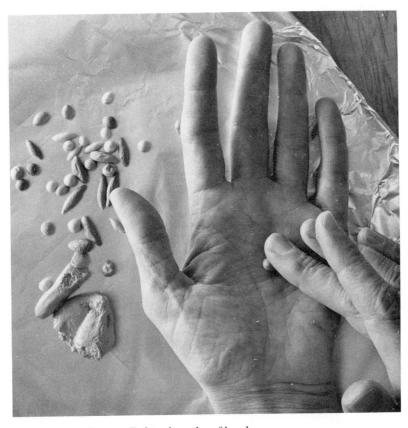

Fig. 4–10 Beads are rolled in the palm of hand.

Stringing Beads

1. Thread a medium-sized needle with a piece of dental floss several inches longer than the necklace you plan to make.

2. Begin stringing the necklace by sticking the needle through a bead, then sliding the bead down the string to about 2 inches from the end (fig. 4–11). Do not knot the string or press the beads too tightly together.

3. For a random arrangement of colors, stir the beads of different colors together. Set a handful to one side and string these beads first, disregarding which colors fall next to one another. Repeat this with small piles of beads until all are strung, and you will avoid a self-conscious color arrangement. (Oval-shaped beads may be threaded lengthwise or through one end for a teardrop effect.)

4. When enough beads have been strung to form a necklace, leave string ends untied and return the necklace to the oven for 5 or 10 more minutes at 325°, or until the beads are completely baked. Pinch one of the largest to make certain the center is hard. Overbaking will dull the colors.

Tube Beads

1. To make tube beads, pat out a piece of dough about ¼" thick. Press a plastic drinking straw into the flattened dough piece. Give it a twist to pick up the dough in the end of the straw. Repeat until dough fills about 2" in the end of the straw.

2. Holding the dough-filled end of the straw over a foil-covered cookie sheet, press the straw tightly between thumb and forefinger just above the dough-filled section. Squeeze the dough from the straw onto the foil, as you would toothpaste from

Fig. 4–11 A medium-sized needle is used to string the beads on dental floss.

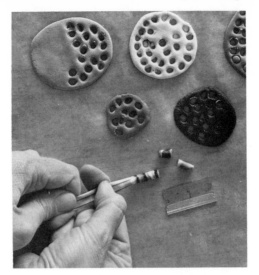

← fantastic-looking

Fig. 4–12 Layered dough is squeezed from a straw for tube beads.

a tube. Slice it into ½″ sections with a sharp razor blade. Separate the sections carefully, patting the ends to smooth any distortions.

3. To make multicolored, striped tube beads, follow the steps above using several colors of dough (fig. 4–12). Pat a small amount of dough of each color into flat circles. Press the straw through the different colors at random or in whatever order you choose. Wide stripes can be made by pressing the straw into the same color dough several times in succession. Change straws frequently, setting used straws in a glass or water to soak for reuse later. Straws may be cut in half and all four ends may be used.

4. Bake the tube beads about 5 minutes at 325° or until an outside crust is formed, but the center still feels soft. Watch timing carefully or the beads may get too hard to pierce for stringing.

5. Remove the beads from the oven and cool a few minutes before stringing. Stringing need not be done immediately but should be done within a few hours. Be sure to return the beads to the oven to finish baking for 5 to 10 minutes at 325° after stringing is completed so that the beads will be hard all the way through.

Spraying and Tying

1. When the beads are strung and rebaked, check their placement to make sure they are not too crowded on the string. This could cause the necklace to look stiff and wiry. Be sure no gaps remain between the beads, letting the string show.

2. Tie the ends of the string together with a tight double knot

Fig. 4–13 A clasp is tied to a string of beads.

and cut off the excess. Lay the necklace on a clean sheet of paper and spray with a clear acrylic spray, following the directions on the can. When the spray is dry, turn the necklace over and spray the other side. Give the necklace a second coat when it is dry.

3. For short necklaces, tie the string ends to a clasp (fig. 4–13), available at craft supply shops.

LARGE BEADS TO COMBINE WITH FIBERS

Fat leathery dough beads and imprinted medallions are combined with natural fibers in this cascade of jute and feathers (fig. 4–14) by Barbara Morriss, a home economist and crafts teacher from Pacific Grove, California. The hanging is developed from strands of wrapped jute that have been coiled and twisted into the interesting shape at the top. Then she hung rusty-colored, brushed jute from the feathery nest in the center. The instructions below are for making the large beads. Use them to add accent and interest to your own macrame, weaving, or fiber projects.

Materials

one batch of baker's clay	sugar
salad oil	water
aluminum foil	clear acrylic spray
several pencils	wood stain

Instructions

1. Make one batch of baker's clay, using the recipe at the beginning of this chapter.

Fig. 4–14 Jute wrapping by Barbara Morriss is made of fibers and feathers combined with baker's clay beads and medallions.

2. Cover a pencil shaft with a piece of aluminum foil. Wipe it with salad oil.

3. Form a bead about an inch wide, and two inches long over the foil-covered pencil, with the pencil shaft forming the hole through the bead (fig. 4–15). Two beads may be made on each pencil.

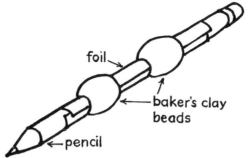

foil

baker's clay
beads

pencil

Fig. 4–15 Fat beads are
formed over a foil-
covered pencil.

4. Mix up a solution of sugar and water in a small bowl.

5. Bake at 325° about 5 minutes, basting with the sugar-water mixture. Remove the pencil, leaving the foil tube inside the beads while they continue baking for 10 more minutes. Baste once or twice during this time with the sugar-water mixture to deepen the color.

6. Remove from the oven and let cool. Remove the foil tube.

Fig. 4–16 Baker's clay
figure by Aiko Cuneo.

7. Spray the cooled beads with a clear acrylic and let them dry completely.

8. Rub the beads with a wood stain to accent the irregularities and increase their weathered look.

BOUQUET OF ZINNIAS

Materials

1 batch of baker's clay
tempera paints: orange, green, and yellow
waxed paper
aluminum foil
flour
lightweight cardboard cut in narrow strips (matchbook covers work well)

a clean, rounded pencil eraser
wooden skewers
white glue
sandwich bags
clear acrylic spray
spatula

Coloring the Dough

1. Make one batch of baker's clay, following the recipe given at the beginning of this chapter.

2. Flatten one-third of the dough on a piece of floured waxed paper. Wipe orange terpera paint over the surface of the dough. Fold together and knead, adding more paint until the dough is a vivid orange. If the addition of paint causes the dough to become sticky and difficult to work, knead in some extra flour. Place the prepared orange dough in a plastic sandwich bag.

Fig. 4–17 Bouquet of zinnias in vase. Made of baker's clay.

3. Color half of the remaining dough a bright yellow, following the above procedure. Store in a separate bag.

4. Color the remaining dough green and store it in a bag.

Shaping the Blossoms

To make several blossoms or a whole bouquet, duplicate each of the following steps, varying the size of the blossoms and the length of the stems.

1. Working on a piece of foil about 4" square, roll a walnut-sized portion of orange dough into a ball. Flatten this ball with the side of your hand to form a circle about ¼" thick and 2" in diameter.

2. Fold a strip of lightweight cardboard and make a sharp crease. Place your index finger inside the fold of the cardboard strip to keep it spread apart. Hold it firmly with your thumb and middle finger. Press the point down into the edge of the orange disk, cutting out a small notch (fig. 4–18). Repeat this motion all around the edge of the circle. Use a new cardboard strip when the first one becomes too soft to make a clean cut. Wash all color from your hands before beginning the next step.

3. Mixing a small amount of orange dough with some yellow dough to form a slightly lighter shade of orange, form a ball slightly smaller than a walnut. Flatten and notch as before.

4. Lift the smaller circle by sliding a spatula under it, and place it on the larger one, centering it carefully. Cut a small circle of dough from the center of the two layered disks by pressing with a small bottle top or pen cover (fig. 4–19). Lift out this center with a skewer tip.

5. Make a third notched disk, smaller and lighter in color than the other two, and repeat the above process, but do not cut out a center circle. Instead, use a pencil eraser to make a depression in the center, causing the petals to raise slightly around the edges (fig. 4–20).

6. Make as many disks as are needed, depending on the size of the blossom you are making. Each disk you make should be slightly smaller than the previous disk. Press each one down on the flower with the pencil eraser. Place a small ball of pure yellow dough in the center depression.

7. Bake blossoms about 15 minutes at 325° and remove from the oven. Make a hole in the underside of the blossom by pressing it with a skewer. Do not stick the skewer all the way through the blossom. Return it to the oven and bake 15 minutes more at 325° or until hard. Overbaking will dull colors so watch timing carefully.

Fig. 4–18 A dough circle is notched with a folded strip of cardboard.

Fig. 4–19 A pen top is used to cut a hole through the first two layers of flower petals.

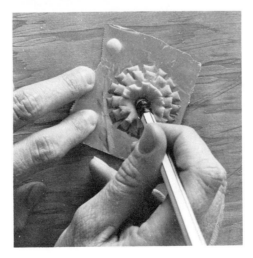

Fig. 4–20 A rounded eraser presses succeeding layers into the depression.

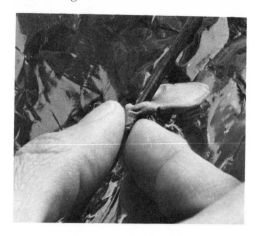

Fig. 4–21 The base of a dough leaf is pinched around a dowel stem.

Formation of Leaves

1. Stain 12-½" wooden skewers a dark green, using felt pen or green tempera mixed with a little white glue. Stand them in a glass to dry. Color one skewer for each flower and then color a few more to be used to make leafy spikes.

2. For easy handling, work each stem on a separate strip of foil on a cookie sheet. Form sausage-shaped pieces of green dough 1" to 2" long. Pinch the lower end of the dough around the skewer and shape the upper end into a leaf pointing up toward the flat end of the skewer (fig. 4–21). Put as many leaves on each skewer as you wish.

3. Use a spoon handle to draw lines down the centers of the leaves and bake them at 325° for about 10 minutes or until hard.

4. Large leaves are made of sausage-shaped pieces of dough about 10" long and 2" wide at the widest part. These leaves are not attached to a skewer; they are simply put into the vase along with the skewered flowers. Each leaf is formed on an individual strip of foil. Leaves may be given realistic shapes by twisting these foil strips or bending them slightly before baking. Bake the larger leaves 15 to 20 minutes at 325°. Remove foil strips from the leaves *after* baking.

Assembling Flowers

1. Use the sharp end of a skewer to reopen the hole on the underside of the blossom if it has closed during the baking process.

2. Lay the blossoms face down. Dip the flat end of the skewer in white glue; then place it firmly in the center hole (fig. 4–22), again being careful not to dislodge the center piece on the other side.

3. Keeping the blossoms face down, lean the stems against the edge of a bowl to keep them straight while they dry.

Fig. 4–22 A stem is
inserted into glue-filled hole
in the completed blossom.

Spraying

Cover the leaves and blossoms with two coats of clear acrylic
spray following the directions on the can. When the flowers are
dry, arrange them in a container of your choice or make a dough
vase by following the instructions given below.

DOUGH VASE

Materials

1 batch baker's clay
glass jar, about 5½" tall and
    4" in diameter
brown tempera paint
foil-covered cookie sheet

flour
wagon-wheel macaroni or
    stamp for imprinting design
small tube-shaped macaroni

Instructions

1. Make a batch of baker's clay, following recipe given at the
beginning of this chapter.

2. Break off a piece of dough about the size of a golf ball. Mix
a small amount of white tempera into this dough, kneading
thoroughly. Color the remaining dough brown (follow the procedure for coloring dough on page 69).

3. Cover the jar with brown dough by flattening small pieces
against the glass (fig. 4–23). Press hard with the side of your
hand to erase seams and smooth the dough. Don't worry about
slight irregularities. These heighten the handmade look and increase its appeal. Fold the dough over the lip edge of the jar and
pat it smooth. Wash all traces of brown paint from your hands
before using the white dough.

Fig. 4–23 Dough is pressed onto a glass jar.

4. Pinch off a small piece of white dough, roll it into a ball, and flatten it into a thin disk about an inch in diameter. Press the disk against the dough-covered jar. Repeat this process, scattering white disks at random over the jar. Use a wagon-wheel macaroni to press into the white disks, leaving a wagon-wheel imprint in the dough (fig. 4–24).

5. Repeat with smaller white dots, positioning them over the remaining open brown areas of the jar. Press each small dot with a tube macaroni to seal it to the brown background and to give it a design.

6. Bake the vase on a foil-covered cookie sheet for about half an hour at 325° or until it feels completely hard.

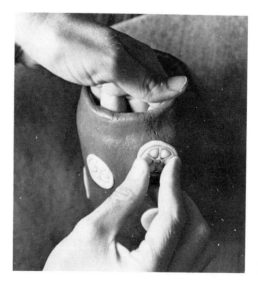

Fig. 4–24 A wagon-wheel macaroni gives texture to polka dots on the vase.

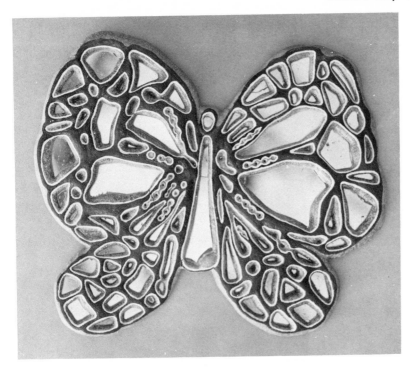

Fig. 4–25 Mosaic made by deeply imbedding irregularly shaped pieces of mirror in baker's clay. It is painted with acrylics.

BREAD BASKET

Materials

1 batch of baker's clay
aluminum foil
oven-proof, medium-sized mixing bowl
cookie sheet

rolling pin
stamp for imprinting designs
acrylic coating, spray or brush on
kitchen knife

Instructions

1. Invert the bowl on a foil-covered cookie sheet. Smooth foil over the entire bowl and allow it to extend onto the cookie sheet. This keeps any dough from squeezing under the edge of the bowl during the construction of the basket.

2. Look around you and choose an object to use for imprinting designs on the basket. The basket pictured was stamped with a eucalyptus pod.

3. Mix up a batch of baker's clay. Knead it until smooth. The dough for this project should be as dry as possible but still pliable and elastic.

Fig. 4–26 Bread basket. Made of baker's clay (see also color section).

4. To make the edging on the basket, roll the batch of dough into a ¼″ thick rectangle. Using a kitchen knife, cut 2 lengthwise strips each 1½″ wide. Join these two strips by moistening the two ends slightly and pressing them together firmly. Gently lay the long strip around the lip of the bowl to form an edging (fig. 4–27). Seal the ends together.

5. Reroll the remaining dough into a rectangle ⅛″ to ¼″ thick. Cut as many ¾″ wide strips as possible lengthwise. You will eventually have to reroll the scraps to finish the basket.

6. Lay three of the longest strips across the center of the bowl in one direction. Weave in three strips in the opposite direction (fig. 4–28).

7. Weave one more strip along each side of the first three strips placed across the bowl.

8. Weave one more strip along each side of the second three placed across the bowl. There will be a total of ten strips, five going in each direction.

9. Imprint the cross joints of the strips with whatever stamp you have chosen. This technique is a help when you are adding the strips from step 7 on the sloping side of the bowl since the imprinting holds the strips in position (fig. 4–29).

Fig. 4–27 The basket edging is lifted into place.

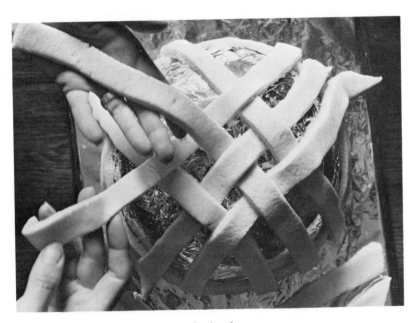

Fig. 4–28 Strips are woven across the bowl.

10. Trim the ends of the strips to extend about ¾″ over the edging (fig. 4–30). Imprint each strip end with your stamp.

11. Place the basket, still on the cookie sheet, in a 325° oven for one hour or until the basket is browned. Remove the cookie sheet from the oven. Lift the foil and the basket from the bowl while it is still warm. Remove the bowl from the cookie sheet.

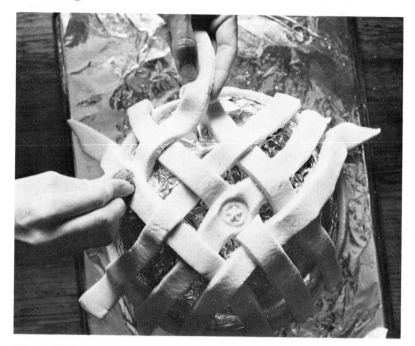

Fig. 4–29 Stamping cross joints helps keep strips in place on the sloping sides of the bowl.

Fig. 4–30 The ends of the dough strips are trimmed evenly before stamping.

12. Now, remove the foil from the basket and replace the basket on the cookie sheet, right side up. Put it back in the 325° oven to allow the inside to dry a bit more. If the basket is already very brown, lower the oven temperature to 250° and watch it very carefully.

Fig. 4–31 Wolfhound by Regina Moritz. The dog was molded of baker's clay and airdried. His shaggy coat was formed by squeezing dough through a garlic press.

13. Remove basket and allow it to cool thoroughly.

14. Spray the basket with several light coats of clear acrylic, or brush on a protective coating. Be sure to coat all the edges and crevices carefully. This will keep the basket from absorbing moisture from the air and will allow you to wipe it clean with a damp cloth. Brush-on varnish could also be used as a protective coating.

HEN AND CHICK PLAQUE

Materials

1 batch of baker's clay
flour
food coloring: red and yellow
clear acrylic spray
bamboo skewer or toothpick
aluminum foil

plastic bag
cookie sheet
vegetable peeler
salad plate with smooth edge
kitchen knife

Instructions

1. Make a batch of baker's clay, following the recipe given at the beginning of this chapter. Form the dough into a smooth ball.

Fig. 4–32 Hen and chick plaque, formed of baker's clay. The details are made of dough tinted with food coloring (see also color section).

2. Working on a large piece of foil, roll half of the dough into a circle about ¼″ thick. Store the remaining dough in a plastic bag until you are ready to use it.

3. Invert the salad plate on the dough. Using a kitchen knife, trim around the edge of the plate. Remove the excess dough and lift the foil on which the dough is resting onto a cookie sheet.

4. Using the remaining dough, roll a rope-like strip about 16″ long. Lay it snugly around the rolled-out dough to form a frame (fig. 4–33). Trim the ends to fit and use a drop of water to join them smoothly.

5. To make the hen, flatten a small piece of dough into a plump, crescent-like shape. Lift the hen onto the dough round and press it into place (fig. 4–34). Using a vegetable peeler, press a feathery design across the hen's body.

6. Roll small pieces of dough between your fingers and pat each into flat, long pieces to form the hen's comb and wattle. Larger balls of dough form the tail and wing feathers. As each feather is laid in place, press in a design with the knife (fig. 4–35).

Fig. 4–33 A thick rope of dough forms a frame around the plaque.

On New Year's Eve, unmarried Russian girls tell their futures with small sour dough rolls called balabushka. *The lucky girl who finds a coin baked in her balabushka will be married within the year. Seven bridesmaids will grind the grain gathered from seven different fields to bake a goodluck loaf embellished with rosettes, hearts, and doves, all of bread.*

Fig. 4–34 The hen is cut out, using the pattern, and positioned on the plaque.

Fig. 4–35 A knife is pressed into the wing to give a feathered effect.

Fig. 4–36 The frame is textured with a long-handled vegetable peeler.

7. Pinch off a tiny piece of dough and squeeze a drop of red food coloring onto it. Work this through. Add enough uncolored dough to achieve a pale pink. Roll a pea-sized ball between your fingers and flatten it on the hen to make a cheek.

8. Pinch off another piece of dough and work a drop of yellow food coloring into it. Add enough uncolored dough to a tiny piece of yellow to get a pale shade. Shape a pale yellow beak and press it into place on the hen.

9. To make the chick, shape a piece of the yellow dough about ¼″ thick and lay it on the plaque. Round the edges of the chick's body so it will have a plump appearance.

10. To form the chick's wing, add three tiny yellow dough feathers, marking each with a design as you attach it.

11. Using a bamboo skewer or toothpick, draw legs for the hen and chick on the plaque and press a hole in each for an eye.

12. Use a long-handled vegetable peeler to create the design around the frame of the plaque (fig. 4–36). The final touch is provided with a row of dots along the outer edge of the frame. Make these with the rounded tip of a ballpoint pen.

13. Preheat the oven to 250° and then turn it off. Using the edges of the foil on which you are working, lift the plaque onto a cookie sheet. Place the cookie sheet in the oven and leave it

Fig. 4–37 Lamb plaque. Made using the same techniques as the hen and chick plaque.

until the oven cools. Slow drying helps minimize puffing of the dough.

14. Next turn the oven to 300° and bake the plaque for about an hour. Watch to see that it does not brown too much. Take it from the oven and allow it to cool thoroughly.

15. Spray the plaque with several light coats of clear acrylic spray to give it a glossy finish and protect it from humidity.

16. To hang the plaque, use epoxy to glue a hanging tab to the reverse side.

BAKER'S CLAY FIGURES

From her fishwife with tonight's supper in hand to her dignified Dickens gentleman, Sharon Spencer's baker's clay characters (figs. 4–38a, b, and c) all possess charm, humor, and a certain self-satisfied appeal. Some are left a soft, bready brown; others are painted in minute detail with vivid acrylics; all are textured and embellished.

Bread was cast upon the waters of the ancient Nile in tribute to the gods.

No special instructions are needed to make similar characters of your own design. Just mix up a batch of baker's clay, as described at the beginning of this chapter, color the dough with food coloring or tempera paints, and make up your figurines. Unfold paper clips so they form S shapes and insert them deeply into the tops of the dough figures for hanging. Bake the figures on a foil-covered cookie sheet in a 325° oven for 30 to 45 minutes, until hard. Watch them carefully—overbaking will dull the colors. Cooled figures can also be painted with acrylic paints. Clear acrylic spray will preserve the figures indefinitely.

ASAWA FOUNTAIN

From the humblest of beginnings (four cups flour, one cup salt) grew a fountain on the steps of the Hyatt on Union Square in the heart of downtown San Francisco (see color section).

Ruth Asawa, a gifted local sculptor who takes seriously the adage that bread is the staff of life, guided the many stages of this two-year long project. Sculpted first in bread dough (fig. 4–39) and later cast in bronze, the fountain is a compilation of talents and viewpoints. As many as 250 lovers of San Francisco, ages ranging from 3 to 90, had the unique opportunity of adding a figure or a landmark or maybe just a cloud to one of the 41 friezes as they developed in Miss Asawa's workshop. The artist, her friends and family, the school children of the city: all brought to the unfolding project their own styles and capabilities

Fig. 4–38 *a*, *b*, and *c* Baker's clay figures by Sharon Spencer: *a)* Madonna and child; *b)* Fishwife; *c)* Dickens' gentleman.

Fig. 4–39 Ruth Asawa, San Francisco sculptor, molds baker's clay figures for a fountain, to be cast eventually in bronze. *Courtesy of Hyatt on Union Square, San Francisco, California.*

Fig. 4–40 Detail of fountain by Ruth Asawa. Sculpted in baker's clay and cast in bronze. *Courtesy of Hyatt on Union Square, San Francisco, California.*

and in the end created a whole that is charmingly coherent and unified.

As a sculpted and baked section of bread dough came from the oven, a gelatine mold was made from it. This mold was used to produce a positive in wax. A plaster mold was then cast from the wax, the wax was burned out, and the bronze poured in. Dough was chosen for this project because the busy relief could never have stood up in the casting process if clay had been used.

The result of this unique experiment stands on Union Square to be admired by all who pass, natives and visitors alike. It is nearly impossible to get by the circular mural with its endless panorama without stopping to identify some of the figures and landmarks: the Golden Gate Bridge bulging with traffic, Lombard Street crookedly descending, a maestro conducting a symphony performance, nude sunbathers in the park, the marina. It is all there—the charm, the beauty, the eccentricities, the industry, the cultural excellence. Most of all, the people are there, parading endlessly through the miniaturized cityscape.

Chapter 5

Fig. 5–1 Imprinted face.
Made of cornstarch dough.

Cornstarch Dough

Cornstarch dough is chalk white and has a fine, smooth texture. It is somewhat less "sculptural" than baker's clay and is most suitable for small projects because of the tendency of larger pieces to crack during drying. (Some large pieces can be constructed in sections, though.) Because of its special characteristics, this dough is a fine medium for detailed and unusual surface treatments—texturing, openwork, color applique, and mosaics. Cornstarch dough is versatile: it can be rolled out between sheets of waxed paper, and squeezed through a garlic press, cookie press, or cake decorator. The dough will keep indefinitely when stored in a plastic bag.

Recipe

    2 cups baking soda
    1 cup cornstarch
  1¼ cups water

Stir the baking soda and cornstarch together in a saucepan. Gradually stir in the water.

Bring the mixture to a boil over medium heat, stirring constantly until it begins to thicken. Remove from the burner when the dough is still very limp and easy to stir. Don't overcook. Turn it out on a plate and cover it with a damp cloth to cool. Knead out any lumps. If the dough cracks or crumbles, add a little more water.

Shape the dough to the desired form on a foil-covered baking sheet. Dry in a warm oven for an hour or more, or dry at room

88

Fig. 5–2 Cut-out cornstarch dough tree ornament.

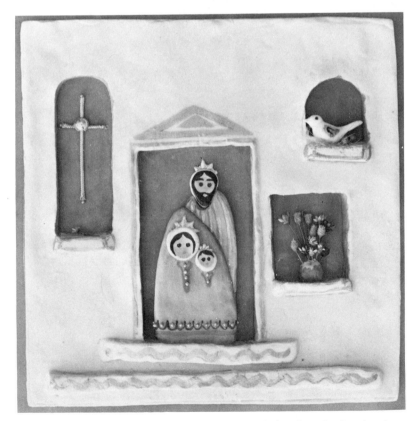

Fig. 5–3 Bethlehem doorway. Made of cornstarch dough with silver beads, gold cording, and dried flowers.

temperature for two or three days. Do not try to remove from the foil until the dough sounds brittle when tapped near the center. Sandpaper any rough edges. If a slick finish is desired, spread the surface with a thin coating of white glue. White glue also serves to strengthen fragile pieces.

Texturing

Pressing one or more objects repeatedly into dough provides a surface enrichment that greatly enhances most dough pieces (fig. 5–4). Have at hand an assemblage of shapes that make interesting impressions. Small gears, keys, even the edge of a cardboard strip—all make effective impressions when pushed into damp dough. Learning to be aware of the texturing potential of the

Fig. 5–4 Everyday objects may be used to add texture, pattern, and dimension to dough.

myriad of objects that meet our eyes daily can be both challenging and fascinating.

Looking to nature for inspiration is of great value when working with dough as with any other medium. Eucalyptus pods, for example, are natural stamps as are many other pods, twigs, leaves, and seeds.

If a particularly interesting shape cannot be brought to the dough, take the dough to it. Key holes, filigree, and sections of ornate picture frames are but a few of the inexhaustible list of sources. Dusting the dough lightly with cornstarch will help prevent sticking when an intricate or deep impression is being taken.

Fig. 5–5 Ceremonial mask, showing rich surface treatment, including texturing, wood inlay, and acrylic detail. Shaped over a plaster life mask, which served as an armature.

Armatures

An armature (framework) is needed when a desired piece is too large to support itself in an upright construction, or, like the Christmas Balls described below, is too bulky to dry fully were the entire piece made of dough. Wire, crumpled aluminum foil, or bottles may serve as armatures (figs. 5–5 and 5–6). Tightly wadded newspaper bound with string or masking tape can be covered with foil and molded into a general shape to be used as a base on which to build a cornstarch dough sculpture.

If reinforcement is desired for small figures, florists' tie wire or pipe cleaner may be used.

Fig. 5–6 Cornstarch dough vase shaped over a glass jar.

KALEIDOSCOPE MEDALLIONS

The smooth clear glaze of these white medallions (fig. 5–7) is a perfect surface for felt marker designs which are "doodled" rather than being planned in advance.

Materials

cornstarch dough	assorted small bowls and glasses
waxed paper	
white glue	indelible felt markers, some fine-tipped
aluminum foil	
baking sheet	cord for hanging

Forming Medallions

1. Make a batch of cornstarch dough following the recipe given at the beginning of this chapter.

2. Roll out part of the dough between sheets of waxed paper to about ¼ inch thickness. If wrinkles in the paper mark the dough, use your forearm to press it smooth.

3. Place a small bowl upside down on the paper-covered dough and trace around it with the tip of a knife. Remove the paper and bowl and cut out the circular shape. Cut other rounds of dough, varying the size by using saucers or glasses. With a toothpick, make a hole for the cord in one edge of the round.

4. Use a spatula to place the dough rounds carefully on a foil-covered baking sheet and dry them in a warm oven. Drying time may be several hours. When the dough rounds feel dry,

Fig. 5–7 Kaleidoscope medallions. Cornstarch dough, glue glaze, and felt tip marker designs.

and sound brittle when tapped, use the spatula to turn them over carefully and complete the drying of the underside. (This dough may also be dried at room temperature for several days).

5. Take the rounds from the oven when they are completely dry and let them cool.

6. Drizzle white glue over one side of each of the rounds and use your finger to smooth it over the surface.

7. Let the glue dry several hours, and then coat the opposite side and the edges.

8. When the entire round has been covered with glue and is dry, decorate it with permanent felt markers.

Coloring the Design

1. Choose one of the light-colored markers, and use it to fill in a circle in the center of the round. Then add a border of the same color around the edge. This is the foundation of your design. You may want to pencil in light guide lines by tracing around a glass. The top of a salt shaker or a spice jar top can be used for tracing the smaller circle.

Kolach, *an intricately braided bread ring, plays an important roll in Russian festivities. Brides and grooms are blessed, the dead remembered, and Christmas celebrated with this festive bread, which symbolizes both fortune and eternity.*

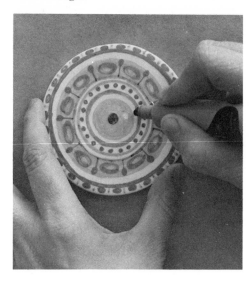

Fig. 5–8 Adding felt tip marker detailing to kaleidoscope medallion.

2. Using another light color, add a ring or a row of dots to the empty space. Rotate the disk as you work, keeping your right hand in the most comfortable position.

3. Use dark colors (blue, black, and purple) to draw narrow borders on the colored areas. Then have fun by adding fringes, scallops, petals, or polka dots (fig. 5–8). Work carefully, of course, but don't despair if the design isn't perfectly centered or if one petal is larger than the others. By adding small dots to the centers of large dots or stems to circles, you will develop a design which is complex enough that irregularities will be unnoticed.

4. Cut a piece of cord about 4″ long. Put a little white glue in the hole and use a toothpick to press the ends of the cord into the hole. If the hole is too small, drip just a little water into it, and scoop out the softened dough with a pin. Then glue the ends of the cord into the hole.

5. Let dry completely and hang on the wall or on a Christmas tree.

CHRISTMAS BALLS

These tree ornaments (fig. 5–9) are simple enough to be a good project for older children, but adults can also enjoy making and decorating them. Very simple designs are effective, and complicated patterns work well, too. Acrylic and metallic paints can be used instead of felt markers, if you prefer. This procedure can also be adapted for making artificial fruits.

Fig. 5–9 Christmas ball. Made of cornstarch dough formed over a foil armature, and colored with felt tip markers over a glue glaze.

Materials

cornstarch dough
newspaper
aluminum foil
baking sheet
large nail
sandpaper

white glue
felt markers in assorted colors, either indelible or water color
gold or silver gift wrap cord

Instructions

1. Make a batch of cornstarch dough using the recipe given at the beginning of this chapter.

2. Crumple a piece of newspaper into a tight ball about 1″ in diameter. Cover this ball with a piece of aluminum foil, pressing it firmly around the crumpled paper to make a tight covering.

3. Flatten a piece of cornstarch dough to make a fairly thin "pancake" and fold this around the foil-covered ball. Smooth the dough by patting and rolling it in the palms of your hands.

4. With the nail, press a hole through the dough and foil into the center of the ball. Remove the nail.

5. Pat the ball smooth again, being careful not to cover over the nail hole. Set on a foil-covered baking sheet to dry for an hour or more in a warm oven, or for a day or two at room temperature. Test the dough by tapping it to see if it sounds dry enough (it should sound brittle).

6. Use sandpaper to smooth any rough spots on the dry dough. Cut a 5″ piece of metallic cord. Put some white glue in the nail hole and use the nail to press both ends of the cord into

Scandinavian daughters dressed in white, and wearing crowns of holly and candles, awaken their parents at dawn on December 13, bearing trays of Santa Lucia buns. Santa Lucia Day signals the opening of the holiday season.

Fig. 5–10 White glue glazes Christmas ball and provides a slick surface for coloring with felt tip markers.

the hole. Add a little more glue if necessary to fill the hole. Let dry.

7. Drizzle glue on the ball and spread it over the top half of the ball with your fingers (fig. 5–10). Let dry, and then coat the other half. Use the glue sparingly or it may drip and make the surface irregular.

8. When the glue glaze is completely dry, use felt markers or paint to decorate the ball.

EAGLE MASK

The construction of the eagle mask, pictured in fig. 5–11 and in the color section, is time-consuming, but not difficult. By studying the details of its step-by-step development, you will find procedures that may also be applied to other projects. You may not have all the tools listed here, but don't hesitate to substitute and improvise. Anything similar will work as well. The eagle plaque is constructed in layers, with drying time allowed for each, so it is a project that extends over a period of several days.

Fig. 5–11 Eagle mask. Tinted cornstarch dough with acrylic detail (see also color section).

Materials

cornstarch dough
tempera paint: blue, green, and red
plastic bag
small watercolor brush
water glass with mouth about 4″ wide
slightly larger glass, or small bowl
white glue
small spoon
aluminum foil
paring knife

waxed paper
acrylic paints: brown, dark blue, and white
2 small buttons or dark-colored dough disks for eyes
assorted canape and aspic cutters
low, wide soup bowl, about 7″ in diameter
bowl about 6″ in diameter
plastic wrap
2 half-inch screws
wire for hanging

Instructions

1. Make a batch of cornstarch dough using the recipe given at the beginning of this chapter.

2. Knead a little blue tempera into half of the dough to color

it a uniform light blue. Color the other half of the dough light green. Put the blue portion in a plastic bag to keep it from drying.

3. Flatten a lemon-sized piece of green dough to about ¼" thickness. Use the top of the glass to cut a round piece of dough.

4. Press out a smaller piece of green dough so that one side is about ½" thick, sloping down to a very thin edge at the other side. Position a spade-shaped canape cutter with the point at the thick edge and cut a piece of dough to be used for the beak. Pinch the lower part up into a slight ridge, and crease this with the back edge of a knife blade. Use the point of a pencil to press a small hole in each side of the beak. (Refer to fig. 5–12 as needed.)

5. Place the beak-shaped piece of dough on the round piece, positioning it so the tip of the beak extends about ¼" over the edge. Press it against the background piece to make sure it adheres. Curve the tip of the beak slightly downward.

6. Using a curved, half-circle cutter, indent outer eye shapes on either side of the beak. Into the lower centers of these shapes press the two buttons or dough disks for eye centers. Make forehead indentations with a small spoon handle. Dry thoroughly at room temperature, then cover the back surface with a thin layer of white glue. Let dry.

Fig. 5–12 Face and beak with incised details. The completely dry face is centered on the second large layer of the mask. A heart-shaped cutter is used to notch the edges of the layers.

7. With a glass or small bowl slightly larger than the face section, cut a thin circle from a piece of flattened blue dough. Press the dry eagle-face into this circle, leaving a small edge of blue showing around the face.

8. Use the point of a heart-shaped cutter to cut notches in the edge of blue dough.

9. Cover the bottom side of the soup bowl with thin plastic wrap. Then, on a sheet of waxed paper, roll out a piece of blue dough large enough to cover the bottom side of the bowl.

10. Set the bowl right side up on the flattened dough and then, by sliding your hand under the waxed paper, overturn the bowl, the dough covering, and the waxed paper.

11. Lift off the waxed paper and press the damp dough down against the bowl.

12. Cut away the dough around the bowl edge and remove the excess pieces. Notch the entire edge with the point of a heart-shaped cutter.

13. Leave the dough over the plastic-covered bowl until it is completely dry. Spread a thin layer of white glue over the entire surface, and let it dry.

14. Roll a circle of green dough about the size of a soup bowl out on waxed paper. Set a slightly smaller bowl upside down on the flattened dough. Cut around it and remove the excess. Lift off the bowl and set it aside.

15. The molded blue dough on the plastic-covered soup bowl should be completely dry. Lift it from the plastic-covered bowl and set it right side up in the center of the green circle. Overturn the smaller circle onto the bowl-shaped piece by sliding one hand under the waxed paper.

16. Pat the damp dough tightly against the curved blue base and notch the edge as before, leaving about ½″ of the blue base showing (fig. 5–12).

17. Set the eagle face, with its blue margin, on the center of the layered bowl shape and press it to make it adhere.

18. Press a 1½″ teardrop shaped cutter and a smaller triangular cutter alternately into the soft green dough border to imprint a deep design (refer to fig. 5–11).

19. Cut enough small flower shapes from a flattened piece of blue dough to place one in the center of each of the teardrop shaped impressions. Press a circular center into each with the end of a pen cover. Let dry completely and cover the entire surface of the mask with a thin layer of white glue.

20. Pat small pieces of green dough into the center of each of the points on the outside margin.

21. Mix a small bit of red tempera into a lump of blue dough to make purple-tinted dough. Pat small purple bits over the

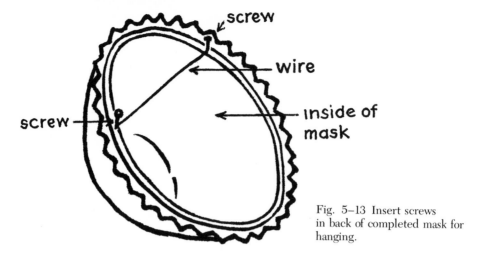

Fig. 5–13 Insert screws
in back of completed mask for
hanging.

green pieces in the margin. Overlap them with a thin "stem" of
light blue, pressing the top of the stem flat so it appears to be
originating from under the layer of notched green above it. Let
dry and coat with glue as before.

22. Paint dark detailing with brown and blue acrylic. Edge
the painted areas with white acrylic.

23. Center eyes with small brilliants if you wish.

24. Use a small drill to make 2 holes on opposite sides of the
inside back edge. Fill these with white glue and immediately insert the two screws so that the screw heads protrude slightly
above the surface (fig. 5–13). When the glue has dried completely and the screws are secure, fasten a piece of wire from
one to the other for hanging.

MOSAICS

Imagine the first makers of mud walls pressing stones into the
damp soil in order to give it protection from spring rains. Before
very many stones had been embedded, someone surely began to
feel a pleasure in the pattern the stones were forming. From
that would have developed a natural desire to enhance and repeat the pattern.

The consistency of craft doughs makes each of them, particularly cornstarch dough, receptive to a mosaic treatment in which
small objects are pressed into the soft dough. Water-smoothed
pebbles and tiny shells have been used for mosaics ever since
primitive tribesmen embedded them in trophy skulls and ritual
masks. Bits of colored glass, used in traditional and contemporary pieces, give a mosaic surface a rich and lively glitter. To
these and other familiar mosaic materials you can add mosaic

chips, or "tesserae," made of dough (fig. 5–14). Flattened bread-crumb dough (see chapter 7) can be sliced into miniature rectan-gles for embedding highly formal patterns. When rigidity of design is not desired, a flattened piece of dough can be dried and then broken into small irregular chips. These shapes are fit-ted together just closely enough to allow the background surface to push up between them and form a web-like network of ridges. The ridges create a secondary textural pattern.

Dough mosaic is most satisfying when used in small areas on a larger piece. The rhythmical patterns that emerge are a pleasing surface treatment. The more densely and evenly the shapes are repeated, the more important the spaces between the tesserae become to the eye. These "negative" areas form counter-shapes which echo their opposites, intensifying the effect of rhythmic recurrence.

Dough tiles several inches square can be made and decorated with various mosaic treatments to acquaint you with the possibil-ities and give you a feel for the technique. The pleasure of mak-ing these small tiles is justification enough for doing them; they are decorative in themselves and suitable for wall ornaments.

In planning a tile, the use of a simple center piece with mul-tiple borders or a radial design will free you from concern about subject matter and let you better enjoy the mosaic process itself. Contrast bands of large with bands of small chips, round with ir-regular pebbles, or borders of deeply embedded chips with

Fig. 5–14 Irregular and uniform cornstarch tesserae imbedded in dough slab.

chips left protruding slightly above the background. Leave some areas free and smooth to give the contrasting texture more power, or make the tile a continuous flow of repeats. Experiment with slight tipping of dough chips to become conscious of the subtle difference shadows make.

Tesserae of cornstarch dough, either small chips or larger shaped pieces, can also be arranged and glued to a rectangular piece of wood as a hard-surface "ground." This gives a stronger, three-dimensional look that can be successful if controlled, but requires more planning than the spontaneous embedding of chips in soft dough tiles. The board can be colored to contrast or harmonize with the tesserae.

Fig. 5–15 Strips of wood veneer were cut with scissors to press into this cornstarch dough mosaic. A tin can lid pressed into the center and decorated with permanent felt tip markers forms a frame for the dough face glued in the center.

Fig. 5–16 Imbedding
wood chips and paper
punch dots.

Wood or Metallic Inlay

Wood veneer or stiff metallic papers can be cut into rectangles or, by using a paper punch, into dots and used very effectively in mosaic dough tiles (fig. 5–15). The veneer or paper pieces are easy to inlay by using a small tool of the same size and shape as the pieces themselves to press them into the dough (fig. 5–16). The end of a pen cover is likely to be the right size for paper punch dots. A rectangular press is sometimes hard to locate, but a piece of eraser, cork, or raw potato can be cut with a single-edge razor blade to fit whatever size and shape you have made the veneer pieces.

A toothpick with a bit of glue on the end makes a good tool to pick up and arrange the pieces without disturbing the dough surface until you are ready to press them in.

In 1540, Don Vasco do Quiroga showed the natives of Patzcuaro, Mexico, how to make a modeling paste from cornstalks. With it they formed a life-sized figure of Christ, which can be seen there in the chapel of the Museum of Regional Arts.

MOSAIC DOUGH TILE

Materials

cornstarch dough
assortment of tesserae (mosaic chips) for embedding: tiny pebbles, shells, broken glass or mirror, or dried dough pieces (breadcrumb dough [chapter 7] rolled thin, sliced, and dried makes light, strong tesserae)

tweezers
toothpick
waxed paper
aluminum foil
rolling pin
5″ x 2″ piece of brown paper
6″ square brown paper for pattern
lightweight string for hanging

Instructions

1. Make a batch of cornstarch dough using the recipe given at the beginning of this chapter.

2. Put a ball of dough the size of an orange on the foil, and lay a sheet of waxed paper over it. Use the rolling pin to flatten the

Fig. 5–17 Mosaic tile. Small dough discs are pressed into a background of cornstarch dough and painted with acrylics.

dough to a thickness of about ¼". Try not to bear down harder on the edges of the dough as you roll it, because you will want the tile to be of uniform thickness.

3. Lay the square brown paper pattern on the waxed-paper-covered dough, and trace around it with the tip of a knife. Remove the waxed paper and pattern to cut the outlined square. Remove the excess dough.

4. With the tweezers, pick up tesserae and arrange them on the dough tile. It is usually easiest to begin with a center piece of larger size or distinctive shape, and then arrange tesserae around it, working alternately from the edges of the tile inward, and from the center outward.

5. When the tesserae have been arranged to your satisfaction, use the toothpick to press them down into the dough.

6. When the tesserae have all been pressed into the dough, pat smooth or retrim the edges of the tile if they have become distorted.

7. Let the dough tile dry several days at room temperature, or place in a warm oven for about three hours. Be certain the tile is dry before you try to lift it, because partially dried dough breaks very easily. Test by tapping it with your fingernails to see if the dough gives a brittle sound.

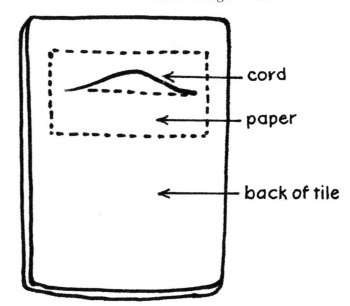

cord

paper

back of tile

Fig. 5–18 For hanging, cord
is pulled through a slit in a
rectangular piece of
paper glued to back of tile.

8. To hang the finished tile, first knot each end of a 4″ piece
of lightweight string. Glue the knotted ends to the back of the
tile, leaving the center section somewhat loose. Cut a 3″ lengthwise slit in the 5″ x 2″ strip of brown paper. Glue the brown
paper over the string, covering the knotted ends. Pull the center
section of the string through the slit, and press the paper firmly
against the tile (fig. 5–18).

PANCAKING OF COLORS

Patting, or "pancaking," colored dough onto a flat dough background produces an effect not unlike a painted design (fig.
5–19). To use this technique, roll out a thin slab of cornstarch
dough for the background. It is easiest to work with a white
background, but you may use colored dough if you wish. The
desired finished outline of the dough slab may be defined as
work begins, but the edges will become distorted during the
pancaking process. They may be trimmed later if needed.

Make your design while the slab is still damp. Place damp
pieces of colored dough onto the background piece. Bear in mind
that straight lines will become wobbles and unexpected distortions will occur in the flattening. (Designs with straight lines or
patterns are not compatible with this procedure.) Rearrange-
ment is not advisable since the colored dough will leave a stain if
moved.

When all elements of the design are in place, cover the piece
with a sheet of waxed paper and pat it until it is as smooth as

Fig. 5–19 This thunderbird tile was formed by patting pieces of colored cornstarch dough onto a damp dough background.

For Easter and Christmas, the Greeks bake a loaf of bread with three petals, which are actually three smaller loaves. Everyone cuts and eats a slice of each of the loaves in remembrance of the Trinity.

desired. Peel the paper away and trim the edges of the piece. A straight edge, such as that of a pancake turner, pressed down through the dough will yield a cleaner edge than slicing with a knife. The pattern is helpful at this point.

Marbled dough, too, can be rolled out and a design worked into it using the swirls and color variations of the randomly marked dough to suggest designs.

PATTED-ON FLORAL TILE

A floral theme is a good choice for the pancaking technique because irregular, "loose" shapes are likely to happen whether or not they are intended.

Materials

cornstarch dough
tempera paint: red, yellow, black, and green
aluminum foil
rolling pin

waxed paper
5″ x 7″ piece of paper for pattern
4″ x 2″ piece of brown paper
lightweight string

Instructions

1. Make a batch of cornstarch dough using the recipe given at the beginning of this chapter.

2. Cover the work surface with a piece of aluminum foil, and then cover it with the sheet of waxed paper. Flatten a handful of white dough on the waxed paper. Cover it with another sheet of waxed paper and roll it to a uniform thickness of about ¼″.

Fig. 5–20 Strips of colored cornstarch dough form stems and leaves in floral tile.

3. Remove the top sheet of waxed paper and cut a rectangular shape in the dough, 5″ x 7″, using the paper pattern as a guide. Remove the excess dough and pat the edges smooth. Recover the dough with the waxed paper to prevent drying.

4. Color walnut-sized pieces of dough in shades of light red, yellow, and a mixture of the two by kneading in a little tempera paint. Color a slightly larger portion of dough green.

5. Remove the waxed paper from the damp dough tile. Roll small pieces of green dough into thin, snake-like strips to lay on the white background as flower stems. Smaller pieces will become leaves (fig. 5–20).

6. When several green strips have been placed on the dough, lay a clean sheet of waxed paper over it, being careful not to smear the colors by shifting the paper. Press the paper down and smooth it with your hand to flatten the green dough pieces.

7. Begin forming the blossoms by dropping bits of the coral, light red, and yellow dough onto the tile, covering the tops of each stem with a piece of colored dough.

8. Using a clean sheet of waxed paper, press the flower shapes flat.

9. Remove the waxed paper and add just a few stems and leaves to give the effect of having some in front of the flowers and some behind.

10. Drop small bits of black dough near the centers of the flower shapes and, again using fresh waxed paper, flatten the additional leaves and flower centers.

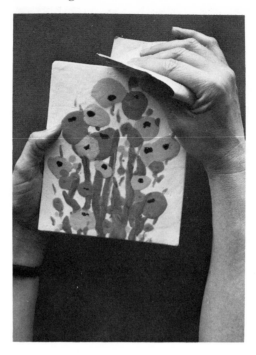

Fig. 5–21 Tile is completed by sanding rough edges.

11. If the composition seems balanced and complete, retrim the edges to straighten them, and let the tile dry several days. When it is dry it will sound brittle when tapped. Gently sand any rough edges on the dry tile (fig. 5–21).

12. Cover the back of the dried tile with white glue. Tie knots in both ends of a 5″ piece of lightweight string. Press the knots against the back of the tile, holding the center of the string away from the wet glue. Cut a 3″ slit lengthwise in the 4″ x 2″ strip of paper. Press the paper down over the string, covering the knotted ends, and pull the center part of the string through the slot in the paper. Press the paper smooth around it.

13. Let the glue dry completely before hanging the tile.

PATTED-ON LANDSCAPE

Materials

cornstarch dough	rolling pin
damp cloth	4″ x 5″ paper pattern
tempera paints: blue, red, and yellow	round cutter, 1″ wide
foil-covered cookie sheet	4″ piece of lightweight cord
waxed paper	4″ x 2″ strip of brown paper

Fig. 5–22 Landscape formed of cornstarch dough tinted with food coloring.

Instructions

1. Make a batch of cornstarch dough, following the recipe at the beginning of this chapter.

2. Color ⅓ of the dough a light blue by kneading a little of the blue tempera into it. Color another ⅓ of the dough green. Color small amounts of the remaining dough light purple (red and blue), green (blue and yellow), pink (using a bit of red), and yellow.

3. Flatten the blue dough on a foil-covered cookie sheet. Wipe your hands clean with the damp cloth. Press the green dough flat next to the blue, and wedge the two together in an irregular hill-like seam. Lay a piece of waxed paper over the dough and roll it smooth with a rolling pin. Lay the paper pattern on it and trace around it with the tip of a knife. Remove the pattern and waxed paper, and cut the outlined rectangle, removing the excess dough (fig. 5–23).

4. Roll irregular sausage shapes from the purple and white doughs, wiping your hands clean when you use a different color.

Turkish breads bear such erotic names as "sweetheart's lips" and "lady's navel," a roll with a dimple strategically placed.

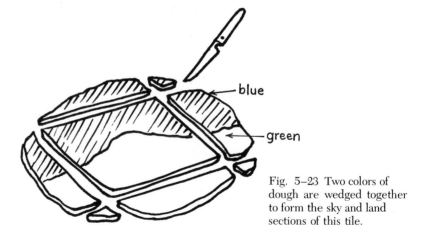

Fig. 5–23 Two colors of dough are wedged together to form the sky and land sections of this tile.

Flatten the dough pieces slightly and lay them on the background to represent other hills.

5. Drop bits of colored dough for flowers on the green section of the landscape, with the size of the pieces increasing slightly near the lower margin. Flatten these flower shapes by pressing them with a clean sheet of waxed paper. Center some of the flowers with smaller pieces of colored and white doughs. Smooth these pieces in the same manner.

6. Use a small glass or other round cutter to remove a circle of dough from the sky section of the tile. Pat a piece of white dough flat, cut it with the same cutter, and insert it into the empty space. Pat smooth, again using waxed paper to prevent smearing the colors.

7. Let dry for several days. Coat the surface with white glue and let dry until clear.

8. Tie a double knot in each end of the 4" piece of lightweight cord. Glue the two knotted ends of the cord to the back of the tile, leaving the center section just a little slack. Cut a 3" slit lengthwise in the 4" x 2" strip of paper. When the cord ends are secured, reinforce them by gluing the strip of paper over the cord, pulling the center section of the cord through the horizontal slit in the paper. Then press the paper down smooth against the tile back. Let dry thoroughly before hanging.

Chapter 6

Salt Dough

Fig. 6–1 Standing tree.
Salt dough construction.

Salt dough is a heavy white dough with a grainy, sparkling texture. It is very hard when dry and will not break easily. Due to its strength and the fact that it doesn't crack or warp, it is particularly suited for standing dough constructions and can be used for larger slabs than the other craft doughs. It is also useful for forming a strong foundation, or armature, which, when dry, can be covered with a decorative surface made from one of the other doughs.

Food coloring or tempera paints are the colorants most often used with salt dough, but any water-based paint or dye can be worked into the dough.

Recipe

2 cups salt	1 cup loose cornstarch
⅔ cup water	½ cup cold water

Stir the salt and ⅔ cup water together in a medium saucepan and cook till well-heated. Remove pan from the heat. Mix together the cornstarch and ½ cup water and add to the salt water in the pan.

Stir over medium heat until the mixture forms a smooth, workable mass. Turn it out onto a plate and cover with a damp cloth to cool. Shape as desired on a foil-covered baking sheet. Dry in a warm oven for several hours or at room temperature for a few days. Heavy pieces can be pierced from the underside with a pencil if the center does not dry completely.

A Ukrainian peasant always presents a guest in his home with a loaf of bread topped with a tiny mound of salt, symbolizing that the poorest of households will share, even if it has only bread and salt to offer.

Fig. 6–2 An open-work trivet made of salt dough. Cut-out designs were made with aspic cutters. The outer edge of the tile was imprinted with a sewing machine bobbin.

OPENWORK TRIVET

The lacey silhouette of a white trivet makes a pleasing pattern against a dark wall (fig. 6–2). By varying the cutting and imprinting tools used, you can make an assortment of trivets with different designs.

Materials

salt dough

an assortment of small cutters and imprinting tools

salad or dessert plate

2 glasses, one larger than the other

paring knife

waxed paper

aluminum foil

rolling pin

Instructions

1. Make a batch of salt dough, following the recipe at the beginning of this chapter.

2. Place the salt dough on a piece of foil. Cover it with a sheet

of waxed paper and use a rolling pin to flatten it to a thickness of about ½″. Lay the salad plate upside down on the waxed-paper-covered dough. Press it just enough to imprint its outline through the paper.

3. Remove the plate and peel off the waxed paper. Using the outline of the plate as your guide, cut away and remove the excess dough, leaving a plate-sized circular dough piece.

4. Press the larger of the two glasses into the center of the dough circle to imprint a circular line there. Use the smaller glass to print a circle inside the first one.

5. Use the tools you have gathered to imprint a border of designs, and a design in the center. Cut out small shapes between the imprinted designs. Aspic cutters or drinking straws can be used. By pinching a crease in one side of a paper straw, you can shape a teardrop cutter. Pinch three creases to make a triangular shape.

6. Notch the edge of the trivet, using the corner of a heart shaped cutter. These notches are easier to keep slanted uniformly if you keep your cutting hand in a comfortable position and rotate the foil on which the trivet is being constructed.

7. When the design looks complete, slide the foil and trivet onto a cookie sheet and place it in a warm oven to dry for several hours. When the trivet is completely dry, turn it over and peel the foil from its back.

8. Use any of the holes in the design to hang it for display.

LANDSCAPE

The three-dimensional landscape (fig. 6–3) was made with one batch of salt dough. It measures approximately 10″ by 12″. The color, fluorescent tempera paint, is kneaded into the dough, so no painting of the final project is necessary. The salt dough gives the vibrantly colored landscape a grainy texture and dries incredibly hard. Children have great fun adapting this project to their own landscape ideas.

Materials

one batch of salt dough	aluminum foil
tempera paints, fluorescent (blue, green, yellow, pink, orange, brown)	waxed paper baking sheet knife

Instructions

1. Prepare one batch of salt dough, according to the recipe at the beginning of this chapter.

2. To make the sky section, knead a small amount of blue

Fig. 6–3 Landscape made of salt dough with fluorescent tempera kneaded in.

tempera paint into ⅓ of the dough until the color is evenly mixed and the dough is light blue. Put the dough on a piece of aluminum foil, cover it with a piece of waxed paper, and roll the dough out to a ¼″ thickness. Cut the bottom edge square and leave the top rounded as shown (fig. 6–4). Lift the foil onto a cookie sheet.

    3. The three "hills" on the landscape are done in varying

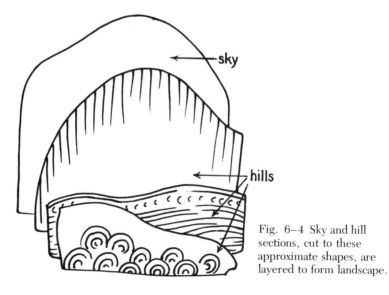

Fig. 6–4 Sky and hill sections, cut to these approximate shapes, are layered to form landscape.

shades of green. Take half of the remaining dough and divide it into three parts. Tint each part a different shade of green. If you want to mix a yellow-green, tint the dough yellow first and add a tiny amount of blue or green paint. If you start with the darker color, it may be difficult to get a bright yellow-green.

4. Roll the dough for the largest hill, following the procedure described in step 2. Using a spatula for help, lift the hill into place on the blue background. Texture it with a knife or spoon handle.

5. Repeat this process with the two remaining hills. Trim the landscape square at the sides and bottom edge. Save the leftover green dough for forming flower stems and trees.

6. Color small amounts of the remaining dough orange, pink, yellow, and brown. Leave a small piece white for the cloud.

7. Roll out the brown dough, cut out tree trunks, and pat them on the landscape. Texture them after they are in place.

8. Roll out some green dough and cut out leafy treetops. Prop the leafy parts of the trees with a bit of dough to make them stand out from the background.

9. Texture and decorate the treetops. Balls of orange dough form the oranges on the tree in the foreground. The tree in the center has bright pink blossoms (tiny balls patted on and textured).

10. Make flowers out of pink, yellow, or orange dough. The flowers on the left portion of the landscape are pink with yellow centers and have no stems.

11. To form the sun, roll a small ball of orange dough, pat it flat and cut rays around the edge. Cut the cloud from a small piece of flattened white dough. Prop the sun and cloud with a bit of dough to make them stand out from the background.

12. The landscape, all assembled and textured, is ready for drying. Dry for several days at room temperature, or for several hours in a warm oven. Do not try to move it from the cookie sheet until it is completely dry.

Scandinavian breads, often dried for the long winter, were pierced by a cow's horn for overhead hanging. When the dried bread had been eaten and spring was nowhere in sight, bark was stripped from trees, pulverized, and fashioned into famine bread. Another surprising bread recipe calls for a mixture of dough and pig's blood. The loaf was dried out over the stove and boiled in the spring.

STANDING TREE

Materials

salt dough	plastic bag
paper for patterns	paring knife
scissors	3 baking sheets
rolling pin	cup of water
waxed paper	tweezers with wide tips
aluminum foil	

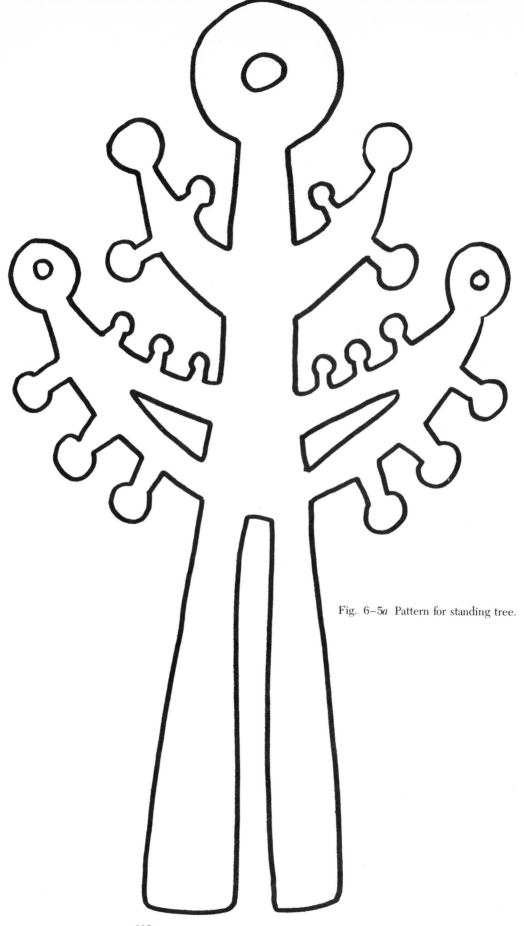

Fig. 6–5a Pattern for standing tree.

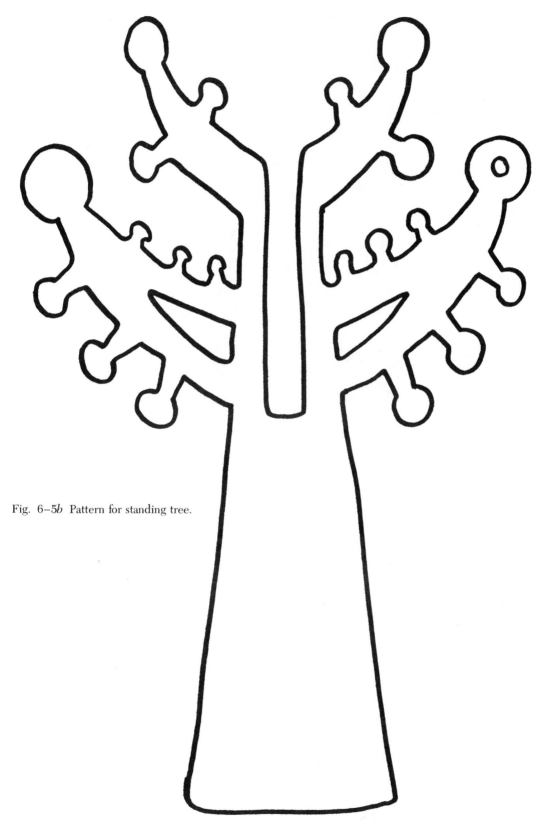

Fig. 6–5*b* Pattern for standing tree.

Fig. 6–6 Standing tree. Slotted construction, salt dough.

Waffles, borrowing their name from old German words meaning "weave" and "honeycomb," are an ancient form of bread. Centuries ago Northern Europe produced elaborately patterned metal cake irons and waffle irons, often heart-shaped and embossed with intricate roccoco scrolls and flourishes. Many Scandinavian families had special irons made by blacksmiths and ornamented with individual designs.

The Dutch introduced waffles to America. It was their custom, in their New York settlement, to present a new bride a waffle iron with initials and the date of the wedding worked into the design.

Instructions

1. Trace the patterns (Fig. 6–5a and b) onto lightweight paper, cut them out, and set aside.

2. Make a batch of salt dough, following the recipe at the beginning of this chapter.

3. Roll out the salt dough on a piece of waxed paper to a uniform thickness of about ¼″.

4. Lay the largest of the two patterns on the dough and cut carefully around it with a paring knife. Remove the excess dough and wrap it in a damp cloth or plastic bag. Use tweezers to get bits of dough out of the narrow spaces of the pattern.

5. Dampen your finger with water to smooth the edges of the cut-out dough piece.

6. Slide the waxed paper onto a flat baking sheet. (Turn the baking sheet over and use the bottom if your sheet has a rim.) Cover the dough piece with a sheet of aluminum foil and lay a second baking sheet over it. Slide one hand under the lower baking sheet, hold the top one, and carefully turn them over.

Remove the upper baking sheet and waxed paper and finish smoothing the edges.

7. Turn your oven to "warm" and put the first dough section in the oven to begin drying. Roll the remaining dough out on waxed paper and use the second pattern piece to cut out the other section of the tree.

8. Smooth the edges, turning the piece over as before in order to smooth the edges on the underside. Put this piece in the oven, too.

9. Let both tree sections dry for several hours in the warm oven. Cool. Carefully slide the larger piece down over the other at right angles, with the slots interlocking. Any "tight" spots can be sanded with a nail file, or can be dampened slightly and then carefully scraped.

Fig. 6–7 These two figures are the work of a five-year-old boy. Bright poster paints in primary colors were kneaded into salt dough.

Chapter 7

Breadcrumb Dough

Fig. 7–1 Flower-encrusted devil. 4″ high. Ecuadorian figure of breadcrumb dough. *Courtesy of Monterey Peninsula Museum of Art.*

The dark-skinned women of Latin America have long used their daily bread for artistic expression as well as nourishment. The soft white bread, torn into bits and kneaded with an adhesive, becomes a highly malleable dough. In the adept hands of Ecuadorian women, this dough forms tiny and brilliantly colored folk figures (figs. 7–1, 7–2, and color section). Devils, llamas, angels, and sunfaces all are generously decorated with minute flowers and scallops.

The same bread mixture is used by elderly women in Mexico to form delicate, lifelike roses, called *flor di migijon di pan*. These bread flowers, dried in the heat of the sun, have an almost porcelain quality and add color and beauty to the Mexican home.

The bright peasant figures and flowers possess such charm that our culture appreciates them as folk art treasures. This has brought forth a contemporary exploration of breadcrumb dough as a craft medium. White glue kneaded into bread pieces results in a dough with qualities similar to that used in Latin America.

Breadcrumb dough is very easily worked, making fine details possible. It is most suitable for small projects, although larger pieces can be constructed over an armature. The dough can be pinched paper thin, sliced, ruffled, cut with scissors, and effectively imprinted. It is probably the best of the craft doughs for beadmaking and small jewelry pieces. Crumbs from fresh bread are a beginner's best choice, but you may later decide to make dough from stale bread, or other left-over baked products. Of

120

Fig. 7–2 Figure from an Ecuadorian nativity scene. Made of breadcrumb dough. *Courtesy of Monterey Peninsula Museum of Art.*

course, dry crumbs require the addition of some water or more glue than the instructions give for fresh bread.

This recipe yields a ball of dough about the size of an orange, an amount sufficient for most projects. Keep the dough in a plastic bag, taking out small portions as you are ready to use them. Breadcrumb dough keeps for several weeks if tightly sealed and refrigerated. Color is added by working in a very small amount of tempera paint. The dough requires no sealing, and can be left in its natural state, and has a pleasant bisque quality.

Before they are dried, finished articles may be painted with glue diluted with an equal amount of water. This gives a soft gloss and minimizes shrinkage. If a high gloss is desired, the dough piece should be painted with a mixture of white glue and water, dried, then sprayed with lacquer. Several coats of lacquer may be needed, with drying time allowed after each spraying.

Recipe

　　4 slices fresh white bread
　　4 tablespoons white glue

Remove the crusts from the bread and tear into bits into a large mixing bowl, or use a blender to make the crumbs (about 2 cups). Add the glue and stir with a spoon until a ball forms. Put the dough in a plastic sandwich bag and let it ripen overnight in the refrigerator.

Rub a little cold cream or salad oil into your hands and knead the dough until it becomes smooth and elastic. If the dough seems sticky, add more crumbs. If it tends to crack, it may need additional glue.

FINGERPRINT ROSES AND ROSE TREE

Materials

breadcrumb dough
tempera paint: red and green
green-covered wire plant ties
fine wire
wire cutters

heavily veined leaf (an artificial
  one will do)
waxed paper for a work surface
florists' tape, green

Rose Blossom

1. Make a batch of breadcrumb dough, following the recipe at the beginning of this chapter.

2. Work a small amount of red paint into the portion of the dough to be used for roses. Color another portion green for the leaves. Use very little paint. During the drying process the color will intensify as the glue in the mixture becomes clear.

3. Form a petal by rolling a small piece of dough into a ball, then flattening it between thumb and forefinger until it is paper thin.

4. Wrap the petal around the end of a wire plant tie, pressing it at the base to attach it to the stem and leaving the top edge free.

5. Add more petals, overlapping them slightly. Touch the top edge of each petal to tip it back (fig. 7–3).

6. Continue adding petals, gradually increasing their size (fig. 7–4). Take care not to push upward when attaching them, or you may push the rose off the end of the stem.

7. If the base of the rose becomes too bulky, pinch off the excess dough.

8. Bend the bottom of the wire stem to form a hook, and hang the rose upside down so the petals won't droop while they are drying.

9. When the rose is dry, use five slim leaves of green dough to form the calyx, attaching them to the base of the blossom with

Fig. 7–3 Curving the tip of a rose petal.

a little white glue. Curl the tips slightly outward away from the rose.

Buds

Buds are made by forming a teardrop shaped piece of dough on the end of a stem. Five narrow green leaves are then positioned around it to form the calyx, curving them upward around the bud to nearly enclose it.

Leaves

1. Use green dough to form a teardrop shape. Flatten it between the fingers.

2. Lay the leaf-shaped dough on the end of a piece of wire, with the wire extending about ⅓ of the length of the leaf. Press

Fig. 7–4 Steps in forming a rose of breadcrumb dough.

Fig. 7–5 Leaves are veined by pressing dough against the underside of a real leaf.

Fig. 7–6 Leaves may be curved by draping them over a cylinder to dry.

the base of the dough leaf around the wire to embed it. Holding it flat in your hand, lay the underside of a real leaf against the dough, pressing just enough to imprint it with a veined pattern. Carefully peel off the real leaf (fig. 7–5).

3. The leaves may be curled by draping them over a spool or other cylinder (fig. 7–6).

4. Lay the leaf and wire stem carefully on waxed paper to dry undisturbed.

Assembling

When the desired number of roses, buds, and leaves have been made and dried, wrap the stems with florist's tape. Add leaves in groups of three (fig. 7–7), then join the stems of the leaf sprigs to the rose stems with the florist's tape (fig. 7–8).

Rose Tree

1. Gather the stems of several rose and leaf branches together as the main tree trunk, and wrap it with florist's tape, leaving the last inch uncovered. Spread the ends of the wires apart to form a root-like stand.

Fig. 7–7 Leaves are combined in groups of three with florist's tape.

During the 14th century when China was ruled by the Moguls, spies were stationed in every household to guard against insurrection. But during the Festival of the Moon, a major Chinese holiday, noble women secreted messages in delicately patterned buns called moon cakes and sent them out as gifts to those who would join an uprising. The rebels, synchronized by the moon cake messages, overthrew the unprepared Peking garrison and the country was returned to Chinese rule. Moon cakes are still sold in Chinese bakeries in celebration of the Festival of the Moon.

Fig. 7–8 A leaf branch is joined to the stem of a rose with florist's tape.

Fig. 7–9 Rose tree. Made of breadcrumb dough.

2. Position the tree in a small bowl which has sides that are straight or are curved slightly inward. Crumple aluminum foil over the wire roots, pressing it firmly into the bowl to hold the tree in place. Fill the bowl nearly to the top with tightly compressed foil.

3. Cover the surface of the crumpled foil with a thick layer of dough in green or brown. Sprinkle peat moss or tea leaves over the dough. Pebbles can be added for an Oriental look.

ENGLISH NOSEGAY

In order to achieve the most delicate tints for the flowers in this miniature bouquet (fig. 7–10), it is important to use food coloring rather than paint. A waxed paper drying rack (described below) gives the flowers the necessary flat bases.

Materials

breadcrumb dough
food coloring: pink, yellow, and green
bowl about 4″ wide
Styrofoam ball just large enough to fit tightly into the bowl
round toothpicks

deep pan or mixing bowl
waxed paper
masking tape
wire cutters
heavily veined real or artificial leaf
white glue
spray lacquer

Fig. 7–10 Fingerprint roses and leaves clustered in vase form an English nosegay.

Instructions

1. The Styrofoam ball should fit into the bowl so that its curved surface protrudes above the bowl opening. The bottom of the ball can be cut to make it fit if necessary (fig. 7–11).

2. Cut a piece of waxed paper slightly larger than the pan or mixing bowl. Use masking tape to fasten it tightly to the top of the pan. This will form a drying rack for the delicate flowers. Use a toothpick or sharp pencil to make about 15 holes through the waxed paper.

3. Make a batch of breadcrumb dough, using the recipe given at the beginning of this chapter.

4. Work green food coloring into half the dough. Color one third of the remaining dough light pink, one third dark pink, and one third yellow.

Styrofoam ball

Fig. 7–11 A Styrofoam ball fits snugly in the bowl and is used to support the flowers.

5. Form a rose of pastel dough on the end of a toothpick. (Follow the instructions for "Rose Blossoms" on page 122.) Slide the toothpick into one of the holes in the waxed paper drying rack until the lower petals of the rose lie flat on the waxed paper. Repeat the process to make an assortment of roses in yellow and two shades of pink. Other varieties of flowers are easy to improvise.

6. Dough leaves are made by pressing a small piece of green dough against the under side of a heavily veined leaf. Peel the dough piece from the leaf and pinch the lower part around the end of a toothpick. Insert the toothpick in the perforated waxed paper as you did the roses. Tip the leaf so it lies sideways but is not completely flat.

7. Set the completed leaves and roses aside to dry.

8. Cover the exposed part of the Styrofoam ball with a layer of green dough, pressing it tightly to the ball. Use a toothpick to press holes through the green dough deeply into the Styrofoam. Withdraw the toothpick with a twisting motion to avoid lifting the dough covering. Make holes to accommodate enough flowers and leaves to complete the nosegay.

9. When flowers and leaves have dried, remove them from the waxed paper holder. With tin snips or old scissors, cut off most of the toothpick "stem," leaving about ¼″ section attached to the base of the flower or leaf.

10. Put a little white glue on the shortened stems and embed the flowers in the Styrofoam, filling the spaces between with leaves.

11. When the nosegay is completed and dry, spray it with several coats of lacquer. This will give the bouquet a satiny finish. For a high gloss, paint the completed bouquet with a mixture of equal parts white glue and water. Let dry and spray with lacquer.

FOLK FIGURES

Materials

breadcrumb dough	manicure scissors
tempera paints: assorted colors	white glue
rolling pin	aluminum foil
waxed paper	spray lacquer

Small Figures

1. Make a batch of breadcrumb dough using the recipe at the beginning of this chapter.

2. Color half the dough a light tan, for the figures, and color

Fig. 7–12 Minature picnic people, from 1″ to 3″ high, are shaped of breadcrumb dough. Brightly colored dough is cut with scissors and textured to form the "fabric" of their peasant costumes.

small lumps of the rest of the dough in assorted bright colors. The dough is colored by kneading in small amounts of paint until the desired shade is reached.

3. Using the tan dough, form a simple figure about 3″ high. Think of it as a fat stick figure, standing or seated (fig. 7–12). Dough hands may be snipped with manicure scissors to form fingers, if you wish. Let dry several hours.

4. Roll a piece of the brightly colored dough between 2 sheets of waxed paper to flatten it for the figure's clothing. By draping the flattened dough loosely around the figure, you will be able to judge whether or not the size will be adequate. The dough "cloth" can be cut with scissors into any shape.

5. You may want to make patterned clothing by pressing thin strips of dough in contrasting colors onto the flattened background "cloth." Stripes, plaids, and other designs can be made this way. You can use the rolling pin and waxed paper to make the clothing piece completely smooth or leave the added pieces slightly raised for the look of applique. Clothing on Bolivian figures sometimes has horizontal stripes of color with sharp vertical knife creases that give the dough a corduroy effect. Any patterning used must be simple enough to complete before the dough becomes too dry to drape easily.

6. Wrap the completed fabric pieces around the figure to sim-

ulate clothing. Press it tightly to the figure where the clothing is to be fitted, leaving skirts or shawls loose at the lower edge. If the dough has begun to dry, use a little white glue to help it adhere to the figure. Overlap any joined sections to allow for the slight shrinkage that will occur as the dough dries.

7. Let the finished figure dry at room temperature for a day or two and then paint it with a mixture of equal parts white glue and water. Let dry, and spray with lacquer.

Larger Figures

For a figure of more than 3″ or 4″ high, such as pictured in fig. 7–13, you will need to use an armature, or support, of aluminum foil.

1. Prepare and color the breadcrumb dough as described for "Small Figures," above.

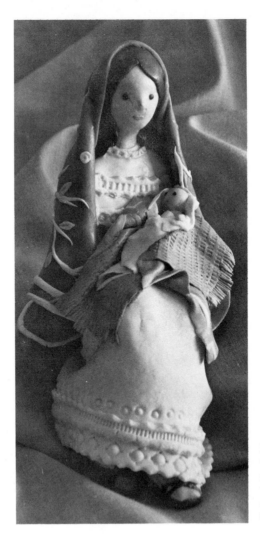

Fig. 7–13 This madonna, worked over a foil armature, wears delicately textured and "appliquéd" clothing. The baby's shawl is fringed by scissor snipping.

2. Form a stick figure of crumpled foil (see figs. 7–14 and 7–15), using masking tape to attach arm sections if needed. The foil limbs can be bent to give the figure whatever posture you want.

3. Cover the foil armature with a layer of tan or flesh-colored dough by flattening pieces of dough and pressing them against the foil. Allow some overlap of the dough pieces to avoid separation and cracking during the drying time.

4. When the entire armature is covered and molded to your satisfaction, add bits of darker dough to make the eyes and

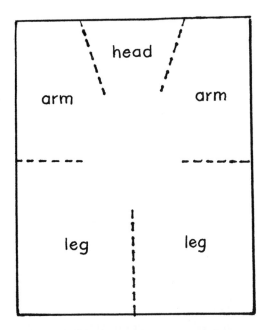

Fig. 7–14 Pattern for aluminum foil armature. Cut foil along dotted lines.

Fig. 7–15 Shaping aluminum foil armature.

mouth. If the hair is to be long, it should not be put on until after the clothing has been completed. Hair can be modeled or made by squeezing dough through a garlic press.

5. Make and add clothing as described for "Small Figures," above.

BEADS

Worn as a single strand or in combinations, beads are a simple yet deeply satisfying decorative element. Breadcrumb dough is a material perfectly suited for beadmaking. The dough is clean and very easy to handle, so it is suitable for lap work while visiting, watching TV, or sitting in the sun. The glue in the dough makes the beads hard and nearly unbreakable; it also tends to make ordinary colors more clear and vibrant, making possible a wider range of color than you might hope to achieve in other media (see color section). Bead colors can be delicate, rich and warm, wildflower fresh, or as muted and lovely as pebbles in a stream.

Forming Beads

Make up a batch of breadcrumb dough as outlined at the beginning of chapter 7. Knead food coloring or tempera paints into the dough to make small amounts of colored dough in a variety of shades that are pleasing to you (see also "Color Systems," below).

Because breadcrumb dough is smooth and easily formed, nearly any shape of bead can be made from it, as well as pendants, either simple or intricate. Variation in bead size is pleasing and a slight variation in shape is what gives the beads their character. If the dough is slightly dry, the bead will be less smooth, with a texture resembling that of potter's clay.

Rolling beads is pleasantly hypnotic. Because the color variations are endless, you may feel content to limit yourself to rolled beads (see color section). By experimenting with a variety of shapes and repeating them in combination with the round beads, however, you can get some very appealing effects. The qualities of this dough are such that it can mimic many materials in color and shape. Look for design ideas in your favorite traditional or contemporary bead arrangements.

Color Systems

You may wish to arrange the beads in a color pattern. This is easily done. The only pre-planning needed is to be sure you

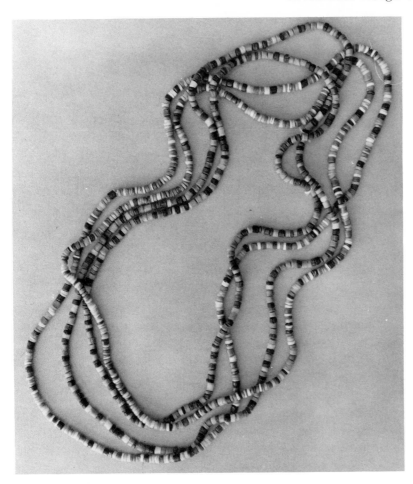

Fig. 7–16 Heishe necklace. Made of breadcrumb dough.

have made amounts of colored dough in the same proportions as required in the repeat pattern.

The following color system nearly always gets good results. Choose a combination of three colors that you like together and color a small handful of dough in each of these colors. Leave a fourth portion of dough its natural creamy color. As you begin rolling beads, make some in each of the three colors, and a few of the natural dough. Then mix small amounts of dough from any two of the colors and roll beads from the mixture. Continue mixing bits of dough together, varying the proportions and color combinations, so that each new group of beads you make will be slightly darker or lighter than the rest, and the color will be changed somewhat, too.

A marbled effect can be made by combining doughs of two colors and mixing just enough to make a swirling pattern. (When

Fig. 7–17 Beads may also be painted with a design when they are dry.

you first begin to work paint into a piece of uncolored dough, you may be pleased with the resulting marbled look, but the veining of pure paint can weaken the beads. It is best to combine thoroughly kneaded doughs of contrasting colors.)

Large beads can also be decorated when they are dry by painting them with any simple design (fig. 7–17), using acrylic paints and a small watercolor brush.

Drying and Stringing

Breadcrumb dough beads can usually be strung about an hour after they have been formed, although the drying time will be influenced by the weather. They should be firm enough to hold their shape, yet not so hard that you have difficulty piercing them with a needle. Rolled beads can wait several hours or until the next day to be strung if they are covered to prevent complete drying.

Dental floss, waxed, or unwaxed, makes an excellent thread for stringing beads. It is very strong, yet fine enough to use with a medium-sized needle. Large needles tend to distort the bead shape during the stringing process.

The breadcrumb dough will shrink for several days until it is completely dry. To allow for shrinkage, a strand should be made two or three inches longer than needed. Tie the ends of the floss in a loose bow knot, and hang the beads to dry. (Large beads should be dried flat on waxed paper. If they are hung, the lower beads may be pressed out of shape by those above them.) Spaces will appear between the beads as they begin to dry. As the beads dry, slide the beads toward the center of the strand to close the spaces. When spaces no longer appear between the beads, shrinkage has stopped, and they can be assumed to be completely dry.

Tying

For strands long enough to fit over the head, tie the floss in a tight double knot. Seal the knot with a dot of white glue before the ends are clipped. Use a toothpick and glue to press the clipped ends into the hole of the nearest bead. If the bead strand is short, tie on a clasp of the kind available at craft shops or jewelry supply houses.

Graduated Size

To make a strand of graduated beads, arrange the beads carefully by size before stringing them. Use the inside edge of a shallow round pan to line them up. Choose the largest bead for the center. Put it in the empty pan next to the edge. Then choose the next two largest to go on either side of it, and continue choosing the two largest of the remaining beads as you work outward from the center in both directions. Similarly, you may string the beads on dental floss by using two needles, one threaded on each end of the floss. Thread the largest bead first and slide it to the center of the strand. Then use the two needles alternately to add the two largest of the remaining beads. Continue adding beads to both sides of the strand until you have used up all the beads and the necklace is complete.

Tube Beads

Tube beads, plain or striped, may be made using the same technique as described for baker's clay tube beads (pages 64–65). Breadcrumb dough beads require no baking.

Heishe

Heishe, or thin disk beads (see fig 7–16) are made with a technique similar to that used for tube beads. Press a drinking straw into a piece of flattened dough, twisting it slightly to pick up the dough piece in the end. Drop the dough piece on waxed paper, blowing through the straw to dislodge it if necessary. Be sure to make plenty of these flat beads so you will have enough for a strand. They will dry quickly so it is best to string them immediately. A narrow cocktail straw can be used to make very small beads, and plastic tubes in which chocolate shot or colored sugars are sometimes sold can be used for making large beads.

Leaf Beads

Leaf beads, as seen in fig. 7–18, are easy to make. Press a flat piece of dough into a leaf shape. Pinch the dough at the base of the leaf to form a short thick stem to be pierced and threaded.

Fig. 7–18 Delicately veined beads are formed by pressing breadcrumb dough against a real leaf.

Press the underside of a heavily veined leaf on the dough to imprint it with the vein pattern. Peel off the real leaf and set the dough leaf aside to dry slightly while making others. String these leaf-shaped beads alternately with round beads to prevent the shapes from overlapping.

PENDANTS

Pendants can be formed in any shape to be used singly on a string of beads, or several may be strung on one necklace. A single pendant with a large hole can also be worn on a chain, ribbon, or leather thong (figs. 7–19a and b). Cookie presses or textured household items can be used to stamp designs on dough medallions. They can be painted or glazed with white glue and then decorated with indelible markers. An unusual stone or small seashell can be worn as a necklace by embedding it in a dough pendant.

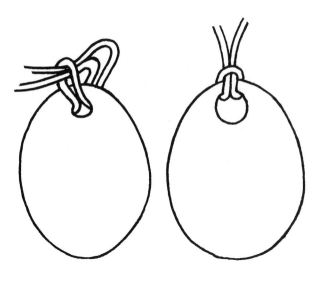

Fig. 7–19 *a*
Threading cord
through pendant
(*left*).
Fig. 7–19 *b*
Pendant
suspended on
cord (*right*).

FEATHERED BEAD NECKLACE

Materials

breadcrumb dough
tempera paint
toothpick
small feathers or the tips of
  larger feathers

dental floss
two medium-sized needles
white glue
clasp, purchased at crafts store
  or jewelry supply store

Instructions

1. Make a batch of breadcrumb dough using the recipe given at the beginning of this chapter. Knead in some tempera paint to make the dough the shade you desire.

2. Roll a bit of dough into a small cone shape. Use a toothpick to press a hole up into the flat end of the cone. Repeat the process until you have formed as many of these beads as you will need to hold the feathers for the necklace. The cones do not all have to be exactly the same size.

3. Roll enough round beads to thread alternately with the cone-shaped beads and to fill out both ends of the necklace.

4. Let the beads dry for half an hour or until they are just firm enough to hold their shape while threading.

5. Thread the two needles on opposite ends of a piece of dental floss.

6. Begin with the largest of the cone-shaped beads, threading it horizontally through the narrow end, and sliding it all the way to the center of the strand.

7. Choose the two largest of the round beads and thread one on each needle, sliding them down next to the large cone.

8. Continue threading the cones and round beads alternately,

Fig. 7–20 Feathers are inserted in cone-shaped beads of breadcrumb dough.

using the needle at one end first, then the other needle, and always choosing the largest of the remaining beads until they are all strung.

9. Tie the ends of the floss in a loose bow knot and let it dry for several days. As the beads dry they will shrink, leaving spaces between them. Slide the beads down toward the center as this occurs. When the spaces no longer appear, the beads are dry.

10. Lay the beads flat on a table to add the feathers. With a toothpick, put a little glue in the hole at the end of the largest cone-shaped bead and insert the quill end of the largest feather. Repeat with the rest of the cone-shaped beads, using the smallest feathers near the ends of the strand.

11. Tie the two ends of the floss to the rings of the clasp. Add a dot of glue to the knot.

BEAD CURTAIN

On special occasions Swiss and German godparents give their godchildren edible sculptures of large and intricately formed breads shaped as men and women.

Bead curtains are easily made for small windows, or as a group project for large windows and doors. Any of the types of beads described can be strung and hung vertically from a rod. A tape may be sewn to the top of the strands to keep the spacing uniform.

Chapter 8

Working
with Children

Fig. 8–1 Horse and rider.
Baker's clay figure
by eight-year-old boy.

Mudpies baking in the sun, cookie cutter shapes cut from pale dough, lumps of clay to pound and press—no child grows up without finding a way to record his impressions of the world unfolding around him. We are all born with an urge and ability to give form to a shapeless mass, to explore the sense of touch. Children bring a freshness and directness to this experience.

Dough, the stuff of folk artists and sculptors, is also for children. It has become an essential ingredient in early art experiences. Mothers keep it on hand for pre-schoolers, and teachers use it in the classroom. It can be pressed, poked, squeezed, and imprinted, dried to a rigid form or returned soft to a plastic bag in the refrigerator for another day.

This craft medium is nontoxic. It can be tinted with food coloring or painted when dry. It cleans up easily and keeps indefinitely. The basic ingredients are to be found on any kitchen shelf and are inexpensive.

No need to dole out walnut-sized chunks for little hands to delicately finger. Watching a child rake up huge piles of sand for a castle at the beach or pat a life-sized snowman into shape shows that children like to work on a large scale. They need generous amounts of dough to mold with their whole hands, to press handprints (or feet), to shape a horse with garlic press mane, or roll in long coils to snake across the table.

Fingers are the first tools of the child. Later, locating objects to press into the dough becomes an adventure, the toybox and desk a treasure trove (fig. 8–3).

Baker's clay is an excellent dough to use with children. Tinted
139

Fig. 8–2 Children working with bread dough.

with a little food coloring, it becomes a bright "clay," appealing, manipulative, and easy to clean up. It also lends itself to classroom projects in varying degrees of sophistication. Left to air dry or baked until slightly browned in a slow oven, baker's clay objects will keep well if coated with clear acrylic spray and protected from extreme humidity.

Cornstarch dough is of finer texture and air dries better than baker's clay. It does occasionally crack during the drying process, however. Salt dough dries hard and strong but is a little sticky, so keep a damp washcloth handy for each child. Both of

Fig. 8–3 Five-year-old boy's portrait of a surfer. Made of cornstarch dough with pebble features and hair formed with a garlic press.

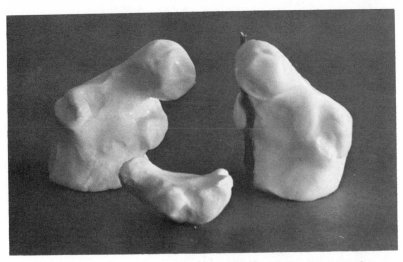

Fig. 8–4 Holy Family by eight-year-old girl. Made of glazed cornstarch dough. (See also color section.)

these doughs are easily cleaned up. Dropped crumbs can be swept away when dry.

Breadcrumb dough is most effective when used to make small objects, so it is probably best kept for older children whose fine-muscle coordination is better developed.

BUBBLEHEADS

Lillian Dardin, an elementary school teacher, uses the Bubble-head project (fig. 8–5) with sixth graders. It could be used successfully with almost any age level. There are two approaches to making Bubbleheads. One is to let the students search magazines for pictures first and then make heads to go with them. Another is to make the Bubbleheads and then go through the magazines to match them up.

Materials

1 batch of baker's clay for every 15 children
garlic press for "hair"
sharp implement (pencil, compass, knife)
aluminum foil

magazines with large, colorful pictures of people and animals
clear acrylic spray
construction paper
glue

Instructions

1. Make up the baker's clay using the recipe given at the beginning of chapter 4.

Fig. 8–5 Bubblehead.
Baker's clay head on
magazine picture.

2. Working on aluminum foil, shape a small head slightly flattened at the back or completely flattened. Eyes and other features may be made by using beads or just pressing, poking, and modeling. Braided or garlic press "hair" may be attached by moistening the head slightly and pressing the dough to be added.

3. Bake Bubbleheads slowly in a 325° oven until dry, about an hour. Paint if desired and spray with clear acrylic.

4. Mount the desired magazine picture on contrasting-colored construction paper. Glue the Bubbleheads in place.

Fig. 8–6 Checker set.
Breadcrumb dough with felt
checkerboard.

CHECKER SET

Hand-formed checkers with a matching felt checkerboard (fig. 8–6) make a project suitable for an older child, or a young one with adult help. The dots on the checkers serve a useful as well as decorative purpose. When a man is crowned, the checker is overturned to expose the plain side. This is easier than trying to stack the irregular checkers to make "kings."

Materials

plastic sheet or tablecloth for work surface
breadcrumb dough
red and black paint, either acrylic or tempera
plastic sandwich bags
circular cutter about 1" in diameter
paper punch
red paper
black paper
pencil or pen with flat round end

toothpicks
red felt, one square foot
black felt, one square foot
white glue

Optional:
snap
needle and thread
1 square foot of red or black felt

Instructions

1. Make the breadcrumb dough using the recipe at the beginning of chapter 7.

2. Color half the dough red by working paint into it. Put it into a plastic sandwich bag to keep it from drying.

3. Color the rest of the dough black and store it in a second sandwich bag.

4. Pat out the red dough to a thickness of about ¼". Cut 12 pieces from the dough using the circular cutter. Pat the edges smooth with your fingers and set checkers aside.

5. With the paper punch, cut 12 dots from the black paper.

6. Dampen the end of a toothpick and use it to pick up the dots, centering one on each of the red checkers. Use the flat end of a pen or pencil to press the dot firmly down into the dough.

7. Use the same procedure to form 12 black checkers. Center each of them with a red paper dot. Set all the checkers aside to dry.

8. Cut a piece of black felt into a square 8" × 8".

9. Cut 32 1" squares of red felt.

10. Use a little white glue to fasten the red squares onto the

black felt background piece. Space them an inch apart to form a checkerboard pattern.

Optional: Matching felt can be used to make an envelope-like kit for the checker set. Fold up the bottom third of a square foot of red or black felt. Stitch the sides by hand or machine. Fold the top unstitched third down even with the bottom edge to form the flap of the envelope. Sew on a snap to fasten it shut.

"ME" DOLLS

Crafts teacher Janie Gamble leads primary children through an adventure in self-image when she asks them to make "Me" Dolls (figs. 8–7a—c). She provides chunks of dough, a few beads, a garlic press, and the invitation to rummage through their desks for whatever else they need to texture clothing and define features. Since no painting is necessary, "Me" Dolls may be made in one activity period, an advantage when working with small children.

Materials

1 batch of baker's clay for each 6 children	garlic press
aluminum foil	tempera paint
beads for features (optional)	clear acrylic spray
	cookie sheets

Instructions

1. Make the baker's clay using the recipe at the beginning of Chapter 4.

2. Divide the dough and tint it several different colors by

Fig. 8–7a, b, and c "Me" dolls. Baker's clay self-portraits made by first-grade children.

kneading in some tempera paint. Leave some dough untinted.

3. Working on a small piece of aluminum foil, form dolls. Use the garlic press for hair. Braids may be made using three coils of dough. Moisten the head slightly when pressing braids into place. Use beads for eyes and make other features using a sharp pencil.

4. Bake the figures on a cookie sheet at 325° for an hour until dry. Spray with a clear acrylic coating.

BABY FOOTPRINTS

What child hasn't done a plaster-of-paris handprint for a mother's day gift? This footprints project (fig. 8–8) is a variation on that theme. The original handprint version also works very well with these techniques and could be done effectively with groups of children. Cut the rolled-out dough into a heart-shape for a further variation.

Materials

⅓ batch baker's clay for each plaque
food coloring or tempera paint
aluminum foil
rolling pin
knife
dinner-sized plate
cookie sheet
ribbon for hanging
clear acrylic, spray or brush on

Fig. 8–8 Baby footprints. Made of baker's clay.

Instructions

1. Make the baker's clay according to the recipe at the beginning of chapter 4.

2. Knead the desired coloring into the dough. Color only one-quarter of it if you wish to make a frame of a contrasting color.

3. Working on aluminum foil, roll the baker's clay to about ½" thickness. Using a kitchen knife, cut a rectangle approximately 4" × 6". Smooth the edges.

4. Hold the baby over the dough. Press one or both feet into the dough, being sure each toe makes its imprint.

5. Using the remaining dough, roll a coil long enough to frame the plaque. Lift it into place. Gently press the coil against the plaque edges to insure a bond. Texture the coil, using a bobbin or other implement.

6. Cut two holes at the top of the plaque by pressing the end of straw into the dough.

7. Lift the foil onto a cookie sheet. Bake the plaque very slowly, at 300°, to prevent distortion. Watch it carefully. If the holes begin to close, reopen them. It will take several hours for the piece to bake.

8. When the piece is dry and cool, spray it with clear acrylic. Thread a ribbon through the holes to tie for hanging.

Index

Kay Gleason. *Russ Cain Photography*   Pat Gardner. *Russ Cain Photography*

Kay Gleason and Pat Gardner discovered a few years ago a mutual interest in sculptural baking and craft doughs. At first they shared ideas, then the authorship of *Start Off in Dough Craft* (Chilton, 1975), and now *Dough Creations: Food to Folk Art.*

The authors live in neighboring California communities. Now a resident of Carmel, Kay Gleason has taught art in Montana and Missouri. After raising her four children, she re-entered the art field as a designer. Her crafts are featured in women's magazines, and she also designs fabric and wallpaper.

Pat Gardner, who lives in Pacific Grove with her husband and three sons, teaches a special education program for teen-aged mothers. She designs crafts projects for national magazines, with quilting and puppetry of particular interest to her.